On the Move: Animal Migration

Robert Norris

rourkeeducationalmedia.com

Scan for Related Titles and Teacher Resources

Teaching Focus:

Concepts of Print- Have students find capital letters and punctuation in a sentence. Ask students to explain the purpose for using them in a sentence.

Before Reading:

Building Academic Vocabulary and Background Knowledge

Before reading a book, it is important to set the stage for your child or student by using pre-reading strategies. This will help them develop their vocabulary, increase their reading comprehension, and make connections across the curriculum.

1. *Read the title and look at the cover. Let's make predictions about what this book will be about.*
2. *Take a picture walk by talking about the pictures/photographs in the book. Implant the vocabulary as you take the picture walk. Be sure to talk about the text features such as headings, Table of Contents, glossary, bolded words, captions, charts/diagrams, or Index.*
3. *Have students read the first page of text with you then have students read the remaining text.*
4. *Strategy Talk – use to assist students while reading.*
   - *Get your mouth ready*
   - *Look at the picture*
   - *Think…does it make sense*
   - *Think…does it look right*
   - *Think…does it sound right*
   - *Chunk it – by looking for a part you know*
5. *Read it again.*
6. *After reading the book complete the activities below.*

Content Area Vocabulary
Use glossary words in a sentence.

current
mate
migrate
pastures
route
savanna

After Reading:

Comprehension and Extension Activity

After reading the book, work on the following questions with your child or students in order to check their level of reading comprehension and content mastery.

1. *Why would the weather cause animals to migrate? (Asking questions)*
2. *What is migration? (Summarize)*
3. *Why do the jellyfish migrate? (Summarize)*
4. *Explain why animals migrate. (Summarize)*

Extension Activity

Think about where we live and the animals that share our space. Do these animals stay all year round? Do they migrate? Create a chart that is divided into seasons. Then under each season add the animals from your area. Next to each animal place a "+" to indicate they stay in the area or a "-" to indicate they have migrated. Add the reason you think the animal group migrated away from your area. Share your results with your classmates.

On the road, looking for surf and sun, let's go on a trip and have some fun!

Moving to a New Place

Animals are not always able to stay in the same place. Many animals move with the seasons, the weather, or to find food.

Zebras

Snow Geese

When animals move to find better living conditions it is called migration. Whether by land, sea, or air, animals **migrate** for their survival.

Wildebeest

A massive herd of one million wildebeests travels across the **savanna**. Thousands of zebras and gazelles follow them on their 1,000-mile (1,609-kilometer) trek.

Wildebeests

The wildebeests go in search of water and greener **pastures**. They survive by migrating.

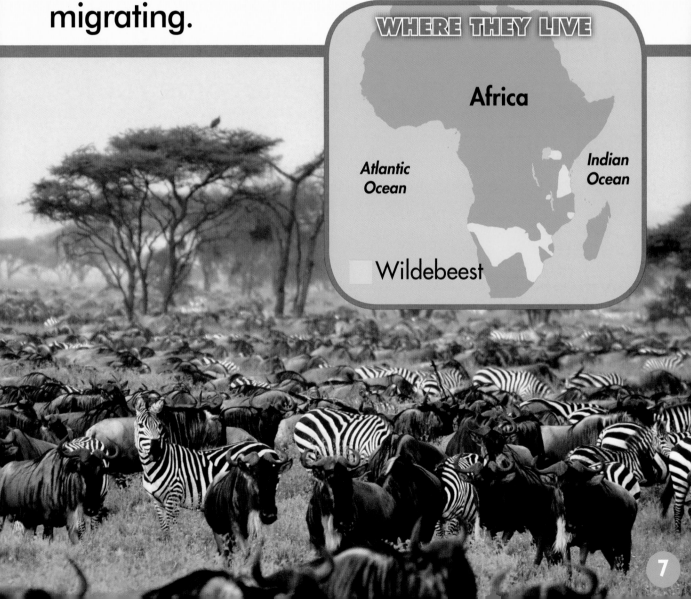

WHERE THEY LIVE

Africa

Atlantic Ocean

Indian Ocean

Wildebeest

Geese

Honking noisily, geese make their way south from Canada. Flying in a V-formation, they follow the same **route** each winter.

Geese

Geese use features like rivers, coastlines, and mountains to help navigate their migration.

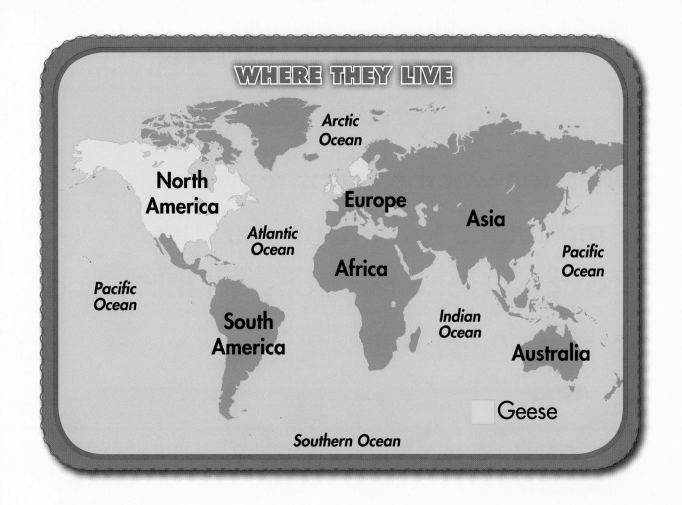

The geese go in search of a warmer climate. They survive by migrating.

Christmas Island Red Crab

When the weather turns rainy, rivers of red charge toward the sea. The Christmas Island red crabs will **mate** and lay eggs in the water.

WHERE THEY LIVE

Asia

Pacific Ocean

Africa

Indian Ocean

Australia

Christmas Island Red Crab

The crabs go in search of a place to have their babies. They survive by migrating.

Christmas Island Red Crabs

Atlantic Salmon

Swimming against the **current**, Atlantic salmon leap across rapids and up waterfalls. The river turns pink as thousands of salmon swim to breeding grounds.

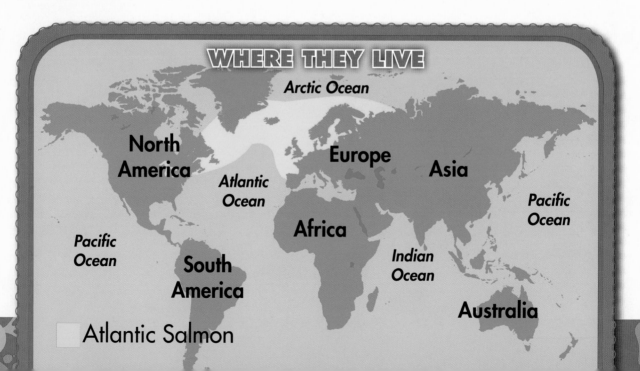

WHERE THEY LIVE

Arctic Ocean

North America

Europe

Asia

Atlantic Ocean

Pacific Ocean

Africa

Pacific Ocean

South America

Indian Ocean

Australia

Atlantic Salmon

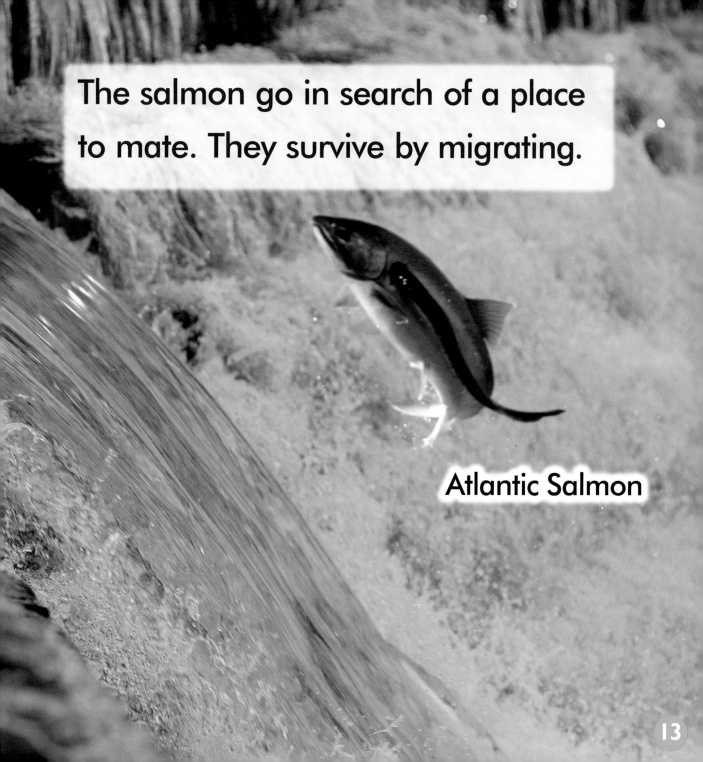

The salmon go in search of a place to mate. They survive by migrating.

Atlantic Salmon

Sperm Whale

The hulking sperm whale leaves the icy waters of the north. He will meet females when he reaches warmer waters near the equator.

Sperm Whales

The whales go in search of a mate. They survive by migrating.

WHERE THEY LIVE

Sperm Whale

Arctic Ocean

North America

Atlantic Ocean

Europe

Asia

Pacific Ocean

Africa

Pacific Ocean

South America

Indian Ocean

Australia

Southern Ocean

Monarch Butterfly

A flurry of black and orange fills the air. The Monarch butterflies go south to hibernate for the winter.

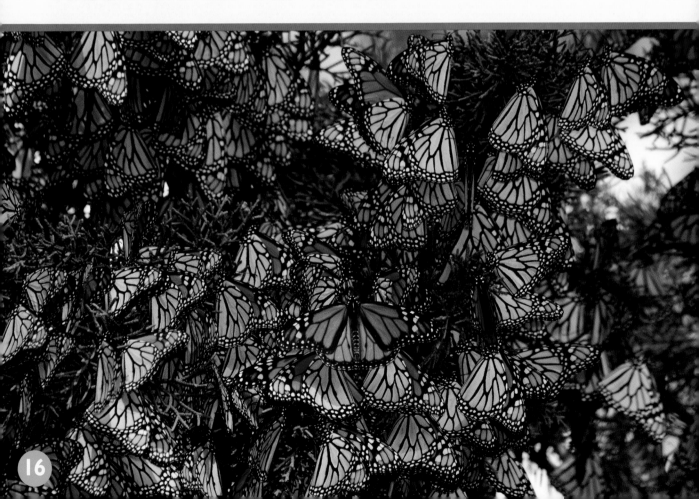

The butterflies go in search of warm weather. They survive by migrating.

Monarch Butterfly

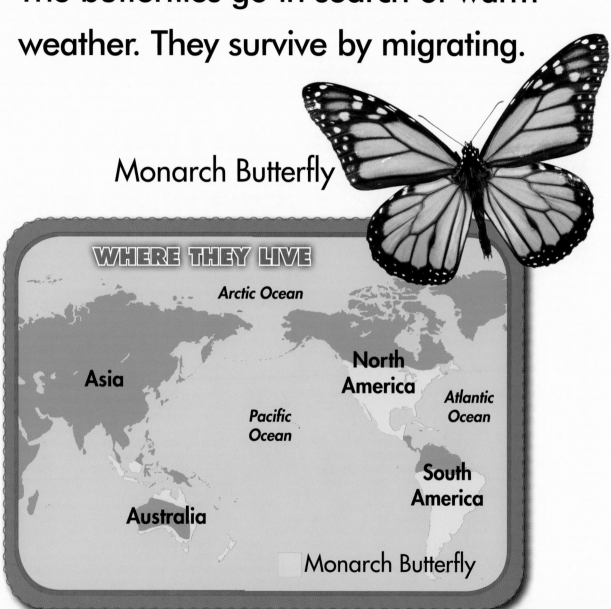

WHERE THEY LIVE

Arctic Ocean

Asia

North America

Atlantic Ocean

Pacific Ocean

South America

Australia

Monarch Butterfly

Golden Jellyfish

Drifting to and fro, golden jellyfish do not seem to be moving anywhere special. Not so! Every day, the jellyfish move with the Sun.

WHERE THEY LIVE

Asia

Pacific Ocean

Indian Ocean

Golden Jellyfish

Australia

Golden Jellyfish

The jellyfish go in search of warmth and food. They survive by migrating.

Albatross

The lone albatross glides on the wind. But come September, it flies across the oceans to gather at breeding sites.

The albatrosses go to have babies and find food. They survive by migrating.

WHERE THEY LIVE   Albatross

North America

Atlantic Ocean

Europe

Asia

Pacific Ocean

Pacific Ocean

Africa

South America

Indian Ocean

Australia

Southern Ocean

Animals migrate for different reasons. Whatever the reason, migrating helps these animals survive in the wild.

Albatrosses

Photo Glossary

 **current** (KUR-uhnt): A current is the movement of water in a particular direction.

 **mate** (mate): When animals mate, they make baby animals.

 **migrate** (MYE-grate): Animals migrate when they move from one region to another.

pastures (PAS-churz): Pastures are land that animals use for grazing, or eating grass.

route (root): A route is the course that animals travel during migration.

savanna (suh-VAN-uh): A savanna is another word for grasslands. Grasslands in Africa are usually called savannas.

Index

About the Author

Robert Norris writes books, articles, and essays on science topics for young people. He lives with his family in New York. Robert hopes never to be caught in the middle of a jellyfish migration!

Meet The Author!
www.meetREMauthors.com

Websites

www.brainpopjr.com/science/animals/migration/grownups.weml

www.kidsdiscover.com/spotlight/animal-migrations-for-kids

www.nhptv.org/natureworks/nwep4c.htm

PHOTO CREDITS: Cover: ©Professionalcreatives; title page: ©Steffen Foerster; page 3: ©gorillaimages; page 4: ©GTS Production; page 5: ©William Perry; page 6-7: ©EastVillage Images; page 8: ©zizar; page 11: ©Jurgen Freund; page 13: ©Anne de Haas; page 14: ©Shane Gross; page 16: ©GomezDavid; page 19: ©Jitinatt Jufask; page 31: ©Josh Anon (top), ©Stubblefield Photography (bottom); page 22: ©Anne de Haas, ©Josh Anon, ©William Perry; page 23: ©EastVillage Images, ©Anita Oakley

Edited by: Jill Sherman
Cover design by: Jen Thompson
Interior design by: Rhea Magaro

Library of Congress PCN Data

On the Move: Animal Migration/ Robert Norris
(Close Up on Amazing Animals)
ISBN (hard cover)(alk. paper) 978-1-62717-633-0
ISBN (soft cover) 978-1-62717-755-9
ISBN (e-Book) 978-1-62717-876-1
Library of Congress Control Number: 2014934199
Printed in the United States of America, North Mankato, Minnesota

THE LIFE HISTORY OF THE UNITED STATES

Volume 7: 1877-1890

THE AGE OF STEEL AND STEAM

BOOKS

THE LIFE HISTORY OF THE UNITED STATES

THE LIFE HISTORY OF THE UNITED STATES

Consulting Editor, Henry F. Graff

Volume 7: 1877-1890

THE AGE OF STEEL AND STEAM

by Bernard A. Weisberger

and the Editors of LIFE

TIME INCORPORATED, NEW YORK

A STONEHENGE BOOK

THE AUTHOR, Bernard A. Weisberger, has concentrated on the study of the United States from the complex Civil War period through the end of the 19th Century. His wide familiarity with the social and literary history of those years is reflected in his works, which include *Reporters for the Union, They Gathered at the River, The American Newspaperman* and a number of essays and articles in professional journals. Born in Hudson, New York, Dr. Weisberger studied at Columbia University and the University of Chicago and is Professor of History at the University of Rochester.

THE CONSULTING EDITOR for this series, Henry F. Graff, is Chairman of the Department of History at Columbia University.

TIME INC. BOOK DIVISION

EDITOR   *Norman P. Ross*
COPY DIRECTOR   *William Jay Gold*   ART DIRECTOR   *Edward A. Hamilton*
CHIEF OF RESEARCH   *Beatrice T. Dobie*

Editorial staff for Volume 7,
THE LIFE HISTORY OF THE UNITED STATES

SERIES EDITOR   *Sam Welles*
ASSISTANT EDITOR   *Harold C. Field*
DESIGNER   *Douglas R. Steinbauer*
STAFF WRITERS   *Gerald Simons, John Stanton,*
Jonathan Kastner, Harvey Loomis, Paul Trachtman, Edmund White
CHIEF RESEARCHER   *Clara E. Nicolai*
RESEARCHERS   *Natalia Zunino, Ruth Silva, Malabar Brodeur,*
Madeleine Richards, Ellen Leiman, Evelyn Hauptman, Jean Snow,
Jacqueline Coates, Barbara Moir, Lilla Zabriskie
PICTURE RESEARCHERS   *Margaret K. Goldsmith, Joan Scafarello*
ART ASSOCIATE   *Robert L. Young*
ART ASSISTANTS   *James D. Smith, Wayne R. Young, Douglas B. Graham*
COPY STAFF   *Marian Gordon Goldman, Ann Shaw, Dolores A. Littles*

PUBLISHER   *Jerome S. Hardy*
GENERAL MANAGER   *John A. Watters*

LIFE MAGAZINE

EDITOR   MANAGING EDITOR   PUBLISHER
Edward K. Thompson   *George P. Hunt*   *C. D. Jackson*

Valuable assistance in the preparation of this volume was given by Roger Butterfield, who served as picture consultant; Eliot Elisofon and Dmitri Kessel, LIFE staff photographers; Doris O'Neil, Chief of the LIFE Picture Library; Clara Applegate of the TIME-LIFE News Service; and Content Peckham, Chief of the Time Inc. Bureau of Editorial Reference.

THE COVER shows the inventions that transformed New York's Bowery by 1895. In this detail from the painting which appears on pages 48-49, electricity brightens the streets and air brakes increase safety on the elevated train.

CONTENTS

1. THE REIGN
OF THE BOSSES

NIGHT still lay heavy on the Pennsylvania farm country near Harrisburg when they shook the big, bearded man in the railroad car awake to read a telegram. It was Friday morning, March 2, 1877. The train had left Columbus, Ohio, the day before, headed for Washington. In the predawn hours, the Congress of the United States had finally determined that the man in the sleeping car, Rutherford B. Hayes, was elected President. He was to take office the next day, March 3. The President-elect took it calmly. He had a reputation for calmness—as colonel of the 23rd Ohio at South Mountain in the Civil War, giving orders despite a shattered arm; as a two-term representative in Congress; as three-time governor of Ohio, his post when the Republican Convention of 1876 nominated him. Now Hayes's self-control remained firm. Speaking quietly to the little knot of men in the car, he asked them to stop cheering: it would rouse the other passengers. The train clicked on, carrying Hayes to the White House, although he had lost the election in November.

Hayes had trailed in the popular vote by a good quarter of a million out of some eight and one third million cast in 38 states. He had quite probably lost the electoral vote as well, though here there was a margin of doubt. Over that margin the nation had been in a wrangle for four months, capped this mad March night when Congress rendered a purely political decision. (A final judicial or historical decision there could never be.) Shadowed by fraud and violence, an end was being made to a crucial election and to the era of

A MODERATE PRESIDENT, Rutherford B. Hayes rests his hand on a document that quotes his political code: "He serves his party best who serves his country best."

7

Reconstruction. A new era was to begin in which the biggest political battles would take place within, not between, parties. These struggles would be waged by tough professionals, not over ideals, but for power and office. The major themes of national life would be economic, the culture heroes of the age men of industry who touched political life mainly through their lobbyists. Post-Reconstruction politics might be described as a meaningless dance to a tune played by an invisible orchestra. Perhaps that is an overstatement, but certainly politics was dragged in the mud at the very start of the era by the "disputed election" of 1876.

IT had all begun on election night when Republican campaign managers, overwhelmed by a tide of adverse returns, discovered that in at least three Southern states—South Carolina, Louisiana and Florida—the results were doubtful. Promptly the Republicans claimed them (together with questionable returns from Oregon) for Hayes, giving him 185 electoral votes, the minimum necessary for election. The Democrats, with equal vigor, claimed the votes for their candidate, Samuel J. Tilden. But the Republicans had a trick to play. The three Southern states were the last remaining in the hands of the Republican machines built in Reconstruction days, so their officials might be induced to deliver a Hayes margin. They did. However, the Democrats had rallied too strongly even in those states for Washington summarily to ignore their insistence that *theirs* were the honest and official electoral ballots. If this claim were upheld, it would give the victory to Tilden.

In December, therefore, Congress had to adjudicate between double sets of returns from South Carolina, Louisiana, Florida. (The disputed election in Oregon was based on a technicality that was easily resolved.) The South was different. There politics had been, for too long a time, bloody and brutish. First there had been the postwar military occupation, when ex-slaves and white Republicans could vote while many ex-Confederates were barred. Then, almost county by county, the Democrats had fought back. Negro-hating poor whites joined forces with former Southern leaders, thirsty for the remembered vintages of power. The party in some states at times changed its name to "Conservative." This was done to attract those Democrats who still remained faithful to the Whig party that had died in the 1850s. The Democrats even wooed some Negroes with promises of better times. Those not amenable to coaxing were threatened; white "rifle clubs" drilled on public holidays in plain sight of Negro crowds; masked riders paid ominous night calls on black and white Republicans. Negroes found polling places closed or mysteriously vanished on election days, and those too persistent in their curiosity sometimes got a split lip, a rawhiding, a bullet wound or even death.

The Republicans, in their turn, had control of state offices and treasuries. They bought judges and voters, black and white, invalidated Democratic ballots by the thousand, used the state militia for strong-arm purposes when needed, and could count on the Grant Administration to send federal troops in a pinch. All this was to no avail; by 1876 Democrats or "Conservatives" ruled eight of the former Confederate states.

This legacy of violence burdened Congress when it met to decide which of the disputed returns of the Hayes-Tilden election should be counted. Some Northern Democrats talked as if they were ready to apply the rough Southern methods on a national scale. Orators at Tilden rallies bellowed "Tilden

Practicing an ancient political art, Rutherford B. Hayes kisses babies in Steubenville, Ohio, during the presidential campaign of 1876. Hayes left most other electioneering to his party leaders. In fact he made very few personal appearances during the entire campaign. Pleased, the New York "Times" observed, "He is not going to talk himself out of the Presidency."

or Blood!" to answering roars of approval. There was fevered talk of a march on Washington, led by the militia of Democratic-controlled states. For the second time in 16 years the United States might have turned from ballot to bullet. The year 1877 was, in its way, as crucial as 1861. Fortunately, it was not 1861 and certain changes had made it possible for men to compromise rather than shoot it out.

For one thing, the Civil War had cost more than half a million lives and one war was enough for a generation. Also, the Republican party was no longer the grand young coalition it had once been. The uplifters and antislavery-ites of 1856 no longer dominated it. The party had grown fat and corrupt in power and its more thoughtful members (among them Hayes) were quite unready to shed blood to keep it in power. They believed, in fact, that the party needed housecleaning; a good beginning might be made by abandoning to their fate the Republican carpetbaggers still in the South, and starting with a fresh Southern policy. This would also mean abandoning the Negro, to make whatever terms he could with his old masters. But many Republicans felt that "idealism" had done all it could for the Negro, that the nation should now get on with other business.

The Democratic party had changed too, particularly in its Southern congressional delegations. Once, the South had spoken for an essentially agrarian point of view. This was remembered by Northern farm spokesmen in 1877, and they had looked hopefully to the resurgent Southern Democrats for help for the honest yeoman. But the Northerners were in for a shock.

The new leaders of the Southern states—such men as South Carolina's Wade Hampton, Georgia's John B. Gordon or Mississippi's elegantly named Lucius Quintus Cincinnatus Lamar—were a different breed. They owned plantations, and wore Confederate scars and laurels. But they also had investments and a lively interest in all phases of Southern industrial and commercial activity. They were not averse to federal aid for the South's infant industrial economy. But they thought it downright ungenerous of Northern Democrats, after helping vote tariff protection for manufacturers and "hundreds of millions to build railroads, canals, lighthouses, navy yards, docks, workshops, arsenals, forts and fisheries," to become economy-minded just when, at last, it was Dixie's turn. These spokesmen of the post-Reconstruction South had done business with home-grown Republicans in their states; they were willing to trade with Republicans in Washington.

"Honest Sam" Tilden, Hayes's Democratic opponent in 1876, was never married, a friend explained, because "... women were, so far as he could see, unimportant to his success." Tilden habitually looked as though he smelled something bad—a suspicion which was finally justified when first he won, then, through Republican skulduggery, lost the fierce presidential battle.

THUS the situation was ripe for a coalition of moderates from both parties. During January and February, two dramas took place simultaneously. The public aspects of what came to be known as the Compromise of 1877 were worked out in Congress. The Democratic House and the Republican Senate voted to create a 15-man commission (seven Democrats, seven Republicans and one independent drawn from Congress and the Supreme Court) to settle disputed returns. The commission's decisions would be accepted unless both houses rejected them. However, through the disqualification of the first independent chosen, and the switching sides of his replacement the commission consisted of eight Republicans and seven Democrats. While it gravely sat as a court and judicially gave ear to arguments intended to determine whether Democratic intimidation had outweighed Republican fraud, its verdicts all went to Hayes, 8-7 on a straight party vote. Each hearing, each decision and each debate in Congress on whether or not to accept the decision consumed days, and the time left before inauguration was fast running out.

Behind the scenes, however, a strategy to guarantee peaceful acceptance of the results was being worked out in intensive conferences. The moderate Democrats, primarily Southerners, would support Hayes's claim to the disputed ballots. Once in office, Hayes would withdraw the last federal troops from the South, appoint a Southerner to his Cabinet and use his influence for appropriations to help the South build its railroads and public works. Since Hayes had once been a Whig (many Southern Democrats, too, were ex-Whigs), and the Whig party had in its time also advocated internal improvements financed by the federal government, the compromise was a triumph for the party, dead these 20 years.

The pro-compromise coalition beat off the attacks of both anti-Hayes Republicans and diehard Democrats. There was a last desperate attempt by irreconcilable Democrats to delay the final official count through a filibuster, but party leaders held the congressmen in their seats through an 18-hour session until the last vote was recorded. Hayes, meanwhile, had boarded his capital-bound train.

To secure the election of Hayes, the presidency had been sordidly bargained for like a third-class postmastership, without much regard to the expressed will of the electorate. Some of Washington's slickest lobbyists, who expected to profit from a Republican Administration, were behind the final deal. Any Republicans who still dreamed of remolding Southern society—and Northern, for that matter—into a just and progressive pattern for all men, black and white, could bid their visions goodbye. But those dreams had been dying for quite some time, and the compromise, like all compromises, at least permitted a re-united people to get on with living their history.

The election deal of 1877 ended an era whose politics had been determined by the Civil War. Veterans, North and South, would still make political hay out of waving the old banners, but henceforth the important election issues would arise, not out of wartime loyalties, but out of assaults on the coalition that put Hayes in office.

The ruling coalition of men from North and South defended the economic order of the day, a fast-rising industrial complex to which government had been giving all possible encouragement. But by 1877, the powerful business groups were under attack by varied forces. There were workingmen's organizations predicting the "pauperization and hopeless degradation of the toiling masses." There were low tariff advocates, and spokesmen for government control of railroad rate-making. There were farmers and small businessmen seeking to raise prices and ease credit by having the government coin more silver. Farmers also opposed the withdrawal from circulation of some $356 million in greenbacks remaining from the wartime issue. Yet despite continued assault, the coalition, which cut across party lines, held firm for nearly 20 years.

President Hayes tried to live up to his part of the bargain. The South got its Cabinet post—Tennessee's David M. Key was named Postmaster General —and the troops were withdrawn, turning South Carolina, Florida and Louisiana over to the Democrats. In 1878, Hayes vetoed the inflationary Bland-Allison Bill that pledged the government to purchase, at the market price, two to four million dollars worth of silver a month, in order to stimulate

Reports of shenanigans in the wildly contested election of 1876 spread throughout the world. A British magazine printed the above picture of "fraudulent voters" being herded into a jail in New York. Actually, historians credit the Democratic victory in New York more to the weather: Many in heavily Republican upstate areas stayed home because it was raining.

production of the metal. (It was repassed over his veto.) In addition, Hayes willingly went along with the resumption in 1879 of redemption in specie of paper money. Most significantly, during a nationwide railroad strike in July 1877, Hayes called out the army—on petition of the governors of West Virginia, Maryland, Pennsylvania and Illinois—to put down disturbances. Where Grant had used troops to enforce Southern Republican claims to the spoils of office, Hayes used soldiers to break a strike. Few actions could have more aptly symbolized the changing times.

Yet Hayes was no mere tool of the ruling coalition. Aware that his nomination had been in part a concession to reform-minded Republicans who had bolted in 1872 to form the Liberal Republican movement, Hayes worked at restoring some sense of ethical responsibility in government. He was not fundamentally antilabor. He expected Southern leaders to honor their word to treat the Negro justly; he genuinely hoped to see a respectable Southern two-party system rise from the ashes of Reconstruction. He attempted to reassert presidential independence by vetoing such laws as repeal of the remaining statutes for federal regulation of Southern elections (he felt he owed that much to the former slaves his party had abandoned to white Southern Democrats). He also vetoed a Chinese Exclusion bill because he thought it violated the Burlingame Treaty of 1868 with China. Moreover, on one issue—civil service reform—he was ready to fight hard. Despite his own questionable title to the White House, Hayes hoped to regenerate the presidency, which badly needed strengthening after the Johnson and Grant Administrations. To do so, he would have to fight the real rulers of his party, the state bosses.

THE state bosses had built a system on the old slogan, "To the victor belong the spoils." They controlled appointments in an age when all government jobs, from Cabinet post to furnace tender, were political. Presidents and governors cleared patronage with these regional chieftains who controlled enough politicians to dominate the party conventions—and consequently to determine a man's chance to be President or governor.

Simon Cameron, for example, built up a machine in Pennsylvania in the 1850s, which he passed on to his son Don Cameron. By 1887, when it fell into the hands of scandal-tinged Matthew Quay, the Keystone State machine numbered more than 4,000 county officials, over 8,000 postmasters, plus other federal workers totaling nearly 15,000 men, drawing annually $7.5 million in pay. All jobholders could be counted on for campaign contributions and to deliver their votes if they knew what was good for them. Money was also raised, in Pennsylvania and other boss-dominated states, by selling licenses, contracts, franchises and judicial immunities to everyone from railroad presidents to sidewalk vendors. This money bought newspapers, corrupted election officials and judges, hushed enemies and kept the whole system in perpetual motion. In addition, it provided a rudimentary welfare service to those poor and needy whose votes could be counted on. Both parties had machines and local elections were sometimes little more than contests between bosses for the right to transact the public business at a good profit for two or four years. Only speechmakers and amateurs got excited over issues.

A number of the bosses, dutifully elected by their state legislatures, sat in the Senate. They were a colorful lot, whose arrogance, power and private wealth was typified by Michigan's Zachariah Chandler. A Detroit dry goods

Lucy Hayes was nicknamed "Lemonade Lucy" because she offered only nonalcoholic beverages at her parties. Because of this, the Hayes Administration was known as the "cold-water regime," and one party guest gibed that the "water flowed like wine." Nevertheless, her charming hospitality, as shown above, won the First Lady a reputation as a popular and successful hostess.

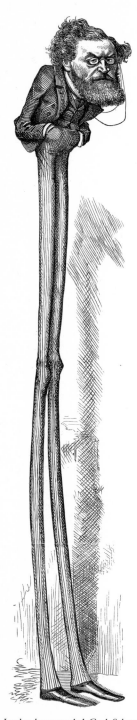

Lanky, bespectacled Carl Schurz, a leader of the reform Republicans who opposed Ulysses S. Grant, was a natural target for cartoonist Thomas Nast, a personal friend of the general. As Secretary of the Interior under Rutherford Hayes, Schurz is still remembered for his enlightened treatment of the Indians and for the start he made in developing a national park system.

millionaire who had climbed the political ladder with the help of his customers, his suppliers and their employees, he was a hard fighter, with no tact or mercy for dependents or enemies. As a radical Republican, he had backed the harshest of Reconstruction policies. His lobby descended on the state legislature "like a cavalry charge," and member after member was dispatched to the great chief's hotel room where, according to a contemporary newspaper, "*by the grace of Zach. Chandler* men were made Governors, Lieutenant Governors and State Treasurers, and by the same royal courtesy . . . became Collectors and Assessors of the Revenue." This regal tone marked his private life, too. When his family visited Europe, they took along four liveried Negro servants, the men in black silk hats and gold-embroidered tail coats prominently emblazoned with a "C." A fitting motto for Chandler and many other Radicals and bosses might have been: "We saved the country and it's ours."

POLES apart in personality from the bullying Chandler was Maine's charming and equally powerful James G. Blaine. A onetime schoolteacher and newspaper editor, Blaine served six terms in the House, three as Speaker, before graduating to the Senate. Gliding tirelessly in and out of committee meetings, battling for Republican orthodoxies on the floor with doggedness but some humor, he developed a silky dominance.

Blaine had the *bonhomie* of an accustomed winner. A formidable campaigner, he could stand in a hotel lobby and, thanks to a remarkable memory, affably greet men, briefly encountered years before, with first-name inquiries about their families. He enjoyed doing favors, and enjoyed even more being well compensated for them. This got him into trouble in 1876. A strong contender for the presidential nomination, he had to face the charge that he had used his considerable influence to preserve a land grant for a railroad, presumably in return for the privilege of selling some of the line's bonds at an unusually handsome commission. Blaine defended himself, boldly "acquired" certain letters alleged to contain the evidence against him, and even read to Congress appropriately edited versions of these "Mulligan letters." It was not enough. Nothing could quite be proved, but Blaine was permanently tainted. In 1876 he was passed by for the nomination as too risky.

Still another type of Republican boss was New York's Roscoe Conkling, a brilliant lawyer, a brilliant orator by the gingerbread standards of the day, and a smashing good-looker. His hair curled, his beard flowed and he dressed his six-foot-three frame in good suits, bright vests and colorful silk ties. Consummately conceited, he held power by a combination of work and forceful will that left little room for warmth or friendship. Unlike Blaine, he was visibly, palpably incorruptible by money; also unlike Blaine, he venomously hated anyone who dared oppose him. Blaine had once roused the dragon in him by referring to Conkling's "grandiloquent swell, his majestic, super-eminent, overpowering, turkey-gobbler strut." In 1880, their enmity was to split the Republican party into Blaine and Conkling factions, curiously named "Half Breeds" and "Stalwarts" by one of those processes which creates labels that endure long after their original meanings are forgotten.

Yet another species of Republican boss was John A. Logan of Illinois, whose dark eyes and thick moustaches swept down in an inverted "V" to frame his swarthy chin. "Black Jack" Logan was an ex-Union general; his strength lay partly in his control of the Grand Army of the Republic, or G.A.R., the national organization of Union veterans of the Civil War. Logan was gifted in "waving the bloody shirt," or refighting the war at rallies. And the men would jostle closer to the platform, remembering Vicksburg or feeling the twinge of an old wound. They would think, too, of the pension check that could mean buying a calf next spring—and go home to vote the straight ticket.

Blaine, Conkling, Logan and their cohorts, working with other powerful groups of Radical Republicans, had been able to bring President Johnson within one vote of removal in 1868. Ever since then, the bosses had been collectively stronger than the man who happened to be President, and they did not propose to relinquish their power. For Hayes to challenge them at all, he had to strike, however gingerly, at the bosses' cherished privilege of naming the appointees to federal jobs in their states. As allies in a battle with the bosses, the President could count on the civil service reformers who advocated merit rather than party loyalty as the basis of public jobholding.

The Republican reformers were a mixed group. Full of conscience and character, they accepted the party's new role as sponsor of national economic growth. But they hated to see the spoilsmen and the corrupters of judges and elections fall heir to the moral grandeur of the party that had led the great crusade for freedom. The reformers were uneasy in the kind of world that a Zachariah Chandler could master and enjoy. Coming from professional and intellectual circles in the Midwest and New England, they were uncomfortable both with the vulgar poor and the vulgar rich. They hoped for public service without power, and economic expansion without plutocracy. If they were not always deep thinkers, they knew what they wanted in 1877: morality in government through merit appointments.

The Grant years had been hard on the reformers, but they regarded Hayes as a friend, and in fact he chose three reformers for his Cabinet. William Evarts, a New York lawyer, got the State Department; John Sherman, brother of the general, took the Treasury. For the Interior Department, Hayes chose Carl Schurz, something of a reformer's ideal. A refugee from the unsuccessful German revolution of 1848, Schurz had been a lawyer, newspaper editor, Senator, charter-member Republican and Civil War general. He was totally untainted by scandal. Though the rest of the Cabinet appointments were routine, Hayes showed by these three that there was blood in the presidency yet. Now he even ventured to get the corpse on its feet.

In June 1877, Hayes issued an executive order forbidding federal appointees from taking part in political activities. This was about as effective as spitting into a gale, but it was only a prelude. A bit later, Hayes requested the resignation of Chester A. Arthur as Collector of the Port of New York, along with one other customs official there, on the charge of connivance between importers and officials in cheating the government. However, the New York Customhouse handled up to two thirds of all imports into the United States and employed more than a thousand workers. And most of them—including Arthur—were loyal adherents of Roscoe Conkling.

Hayes challenged Conkling's power. Conkling thundered that political "parties are not built up by deportment, or by ladies' magazines, or gush!" sneered at the reformers as the "man milliners . . . and carpet knights of politics," and pontificated that "when Dr. Johnson defined patriotism as the last refuge of a scoundrel, he was unconscious of the . . . capabilities and

Shot in the back, President Garfield (above) crumples as Charles Guiteau takes a second shot. At Guiteau's trial his lawyer insisted the killer was insane. But the incoherent assassin was sentenced to hang. He kept well groomed while in jail (below) and even wrote a poem about his execution which he was still reciting after the executioner pulled the hood over his head.

13

uses of the word 'Reform!'" Conkling used more than words; he blocked the confirmation of Hayes's replacements for the removed officials. But in 1878, Hayes put through his appointments with the help of Democratic support.

The result of the battle was a divided Republican party. In the 1878 balloting the rank-and-file voters who, on the whole, seemed uninterested in civil service reform elected a Democratic Congress, and in 1880 the Republican Convention managers gave no thought to renominating the President (who, in any event, had refused to be considered a candidate).

At the sweltering 1880 Republican Convention, Conkling, Logan and Don Cameron desperately tried to renominate General Grant, who as President had proven his ability for accommodation with the bosses. But Blaine, who could not win the nomination himself, was able to block Grant and put over James A. Garfield on the 36th ballot. Garfield was an amiable ex-general and ex-Congressman, pious, well (but not deeply) read—in a word, nondescript. The only colorful fact campaign biographers could find was that he had once been a canalboat bargeman. Remorselessly, they hammered home one theme: "from the Tow Path to the White House." Meanwhile, in order to placate the important bosses who had backed Grant and lost, the convention nominated Conkling's man, Chester A. Arthur, for the vice presidency. In a campaign notable for its apathy, Garfield defeated his equally colorless Democratic opponent, Winfield Scott Hancock, by fewer than 10,000 popular votes.

Garfield soon sent to the Senate the nomination of William H. Robertson to be Collector of the Port of New York. Robertson's appointment was anathema to Conkling, because it had not been discussed with him. Furious, Conkling resigned his Senate seat, expecting triumphant re-election by the New York legislature as a demonstration of just who was still boss of New York. But, surprisingly, Conkling lost.

While all this was happening, a shocking crime had changed the political situation. On July 2, 1881, President Garfield had been shot in the back by a crazy young man named Charles Guiteau—one of a host of disappointed applicants for the 100,000 jobs on the federal payroll. After a long, hot, agonizing summer abed, Garfield died and was succeeded by Vice President Arthur.

The shock of the assassination enabled civil service reformers to push through the Pendleton Civil Service Act in January 1883. This created the Civil Service Commission and put 13,780 federal jobs on a competitive examination basis—a start toward the merit system. The bill was signed into law by Arthur himself, who, despite the panic that some reformers felt when he took office, turned out to be an honest if thoroughly undistinguished President.

So by 1883, Roscoe Conkling was out of politics and a civil service law was on the books, signed by the very henchman of Conkling who had caused such trouble for Hayes. With civil service temporarily drained of its potential as a campaign issue, little was left for the two parties to argue about in 1884. The nation was ready for a dirty campaign of personalities. It got one.

BLAINE'S hour finally struck in 1884; he won the nomination easily. But the stain of boodle remained, and reformers by the dozen rose up. They were a formidably respectable force, rich in ancestors and pulpits if not in votes. They included Henry Ward Beecher, the most popular preacher of his generation; Charles Francis Adams Jr., grandson and great-grandson of Presidents; George W. Curtis, editor of *Harper's Weekly;* Edwin L. Godkin

Formally attired, Republican Senator Roscoe Conkling is caricatured in this 1879 "Puck" cartoon. Tall, with a small waist and enormous chest, Conkling kept in trim by boxing and by walking around the Capitol with stomach sucked in. Ironically, it was exercise that killed him: he died of overexertion after walking miles through New York during the Blizzard of '88.

of *The Nation;* Charles Eliot Norton of the *Atlantic;* Carl Schurz—in all, a host of proper Republicans prepared once more to rescue a dear old lady from the scoundrels who had lured her into imprudent ways. They called themselves Independents, but someone soon saddled them with the derisive name of "Mugwumps," from an old New England Indian word supposedly meaning "Chief." They were soon using it themselves.

The ties among the Mugwumps were loose except for the common desire to beat Blaine. Not all the young patricians joined—New York's Theodore Roosevelt, Massachusetts' Henry Cabot Lodge and others remained loyal and regular Republicans. Neither did Roscoe Conkling become a Mugwump, but he did get a chance for the witticism of a lifetime. Asked by a delegation to campaign for Blaine, he replied, "I don't engage in criminal practice."

T HE Republican split promised well for the Democrats, and they rose to the occasion. Their candidate was Grover Cleveland, a man of great bulk and toughness who in H. L. Mencken's words "sailed through American history like a steel ship loaded with monoliths of granite." Cleveland was a Buffalo lawyer with a contradictory personality. There was the young bachelor Cleveland, fond of late hours, poker, fishing trips, and copious eating and drinking—a "sport" and a he-man. The other Cleveland, respectable and Presbyterian, could work 14 hours at a desk, and his public code of ethics was rigid. Many men of the 19th Century led such double lives, but kept their private pleasures private. Cleveland refused to dissemble. When necessary, he could, would and did tell anyone precisely what he thought.

Buffalo had elected Cleveland mayor only three years before. He had been notoriously hard on grafters who were permitting contractors to overcharge the city. Nominated for the governorship of New York in 1882, he had won by an astounding plurality of nearly 200,000. In office he locked horns with New York City's Tammany machine, refusing to let it control appointments, and sending a series of stinging vetoes to the legislature. Most of them spelled out the fairly simple philosophy that government should be clean, constitutional and cheap. It was not a program to answer the most pressing needs of 1884, but programs would not decide this election anyway.

The Democrats and Mugwumps struck hard at Blaine. They called him a "tattooed man." They found other Mulligan letters, one of them addressed to an official of the same railroad previously involved, in which Blaine asked for an endorsement of his innocence that would appear to be unsolicited. It concluded, "Burn this letter." The Democrats joyfully arranged parades in which marchers set fire to sheets of paper carried aloft on poles, chanting meanwhile, *"Burn this letter!"*

The Republicans were not long in striking back, however, revealing that Cleveland had had an affair in his younger days with a Buffalo widow named Maria Halpin and that he accepted responsibility for her illegitimate child. In late Victorian America, such a peccadillo supposedly made a man unfit to be mentioned in decent homes, let alone elected to the White House. The Mugwumps swallowed hard, remembering that they had, for years, accused Democrats in the main of being loafers, drinkers and lewd fellows of the baser sort. But as one of them put it, if Blaine was "delinquent in office but blameless in private life" while Cleveland was "a model of official integrity, but culpable in his personal relations," they should "elect Mr. Cleveland to the public

Exposed, James Blaine hides his head when tattoos detailing his tainted past are unveiled. At the Republican Convention in 1876 he was called "a plumed knight" who "threw his shining lance . . . against the brazen foreheads of the defamers of the country," but the opposition "Evening Post" said he had "wallowed in spoils like a Rhinoceros in an African Pool."

Belva Lockwood, the first woman to appear on a presidential ballot, was twice nominated by the National Equal Rights party. She was an ambitious suffragette who called for a "domestic insurrection" to win the vote for women, suggesting that there are "more ways than one to conquer a man."

Prohibitionist party candidate John St. John was the son of an alcoholic. He planned to campaign in several pivotal states, but when New York Republicans attacked him, he centered his battle there. Because St. John cut into James Blaine's support, he later claimed the credit for Cleveland's election.

office which he is so well qualified to fill, and remand Mr. Blaine to the private station which he is admirably fitted to adorn."

Mugwumps closed their ears when Republican processions chanted *"Ma! Ma! Where's my Pa? Gone to the White House, Ha! Ha! Ha!"* and continued to work for Cleveland. When he was asked how he wanted the story handled, Cleveland's own reaction was characteristic. "Tell the truth," he snapped.

Cleveland won by the thinnest of margins. He had 219 electoral votes to Blaine's 182, but that was thanks to New York, which the Democrats finally captured by fewer than 1,200 votes out of 1.2 million cast. Pundits tried to explain the results. Some credited the Mugwumps. Others pointed to 25,016 votes garnered in New York for John P. St. John, candidate of the Prohibition party, and insisted that Blaine should have said a few kind words against liquor. A partial answer may be the reported alienation of the Irish. Blaine's mother was an Irish Catholic, which was supposed to be worth some votes. But shortly before election time, a Republican orator, the Reverend Samuel D. Burchard, sneered at the Democrats as the party of "Rum, Romanism and Rebellion." Blaine was present, and his silence snuffed out any hope of capturing Irish votes. There has been little effort to pin the responsibility on Benjamin F. Butler, a chameleonlike politician running on the tickets of the Greenback and Anti-Monopoly parties, who got nearly 17,000 New York votes.

The explanations offered for Cleveland's victory ignore the fact that all the elections in this period were close. In 1880 and 1888 as well as 1884, fewer than 100,000 popular votes separated the major presidential candidates. Only twice between 1877 and 1896 did a single party control the presidency and both houses of Congress; Benjamin Harrison in 1888 and Cleveland in 1892 had working majorities in both houses for the first two years of their Administrations. Voters seemed to recognize that there was little to choose between the parties, and elections were tossups, as likely to turn out heads as tails. The election of 1884 was no exception.

CLEVELAND in the White House gave the country an example of a firm but largely negative Administration. He appointed one of the new Southern leaders, L.Q.C. Lamar, to the Interior Department, and set him to work harassing the railroad, mining, lumbering, and stock-raising interests which had camped upon government land in the West and had sometimes even defied farmers with legitimate titles. Cleveland vetoed bills that would have provided special pensions for Civil War veterans with disabilities too slight to justify payment even under the lenient standards of the Pension Bureau. He plainly announced that he would veto any fresh legislation aimed at the purchase of silver. He favored suspension of existing silver purchase laws. He devoted his entire annual message in 1887 to a demand for tariff reduction; however, a bill to accomplish this died, not unexpectedly, in Congress.

He had the temerity to kill a bill that would have had the federal government give seed grain and so help drought-stricken Texas planters, members of the hallowed small-farmer group. "Though the people support the Government," he wrote, in phraseology beloved by conservatives ever since, "the Government should not support the people." Cleveland was superbly consistent. He would not confer government bounty on corporations, as the Republicans had done, nor would he shower blessings on the laborer or the farmer, as some third parties urged. He intended to give nothing to anyone. It was not then, and is not now a formula for political success, and Cleveland failed of re-election in 1888.

Yet he had given the country a superb example, at last, of a man in the White House who clearly belonged to nobody. Hayes had meant well, in his colorless way, but was remembered mainly for his dirt-streaked and speckled election. Even Mrs. Hayes, "Lemonade Lucy," got more publicity than he, by putting the White House on a temperance basis, and forcing diplomats and other officials to fortify themselves in advance for dinners of state. Garfield was remembered chiefly for being shot; Arthur not even for that. But Cleveland, solid and resistant, had restored the stature of the presidency.

Although he was not much of a builder, Cleveland's Administration did see various constructive first steps. In 1887 the Interstate Commerce Commission was created, which, however feeble, established the first federal regulatory body. A new Indian policy tried to end widespread abuse of Indian landholdings. Cleveland wanted changes in the tariff to avoid overburdening one segment of the economy for the enrichment of other segments. While he was not a Jefferson or a Lincoln, he did end the Republicans' 24-year presidential reign and he did bring life and vitality to the Executive Department. He enjoyed a good fight. He even found time while President to marry a pretty girl 27 years his junior. In sum, he had built up a certain popular affection which would, in 1892, return him to the White House.

IN the 11 years that followed the ending of Reconstruction, political life was colorful but not profound. Congress made stabs at regulation of trusts, currency reform, land legislation and the merit principle in civil service. None of their efforts was firm or as yet effective. The political symbols of the age were the stolen election, the Mulligan letters, the cynical attempt to win one more time with the aging Grant in 1880. The bosses were gaudy enough, but lacked exciting objectives for their energies.

It was different for their counterparts in business. They looked on politics as a game for idlers, and took Senate seats only when their business careers offered them no further challenges. And little as the businessmen thought of professional politicians, the gentlemen-reformers thought even less. For them, politics had become synonymous with dirty hands. They were outraged that national affairs were left to the management of men with few ideas about which to differ; that the parties were largely indistinguishable; that the Blaines and Logans spoke empty phrases in halls where once Calhoun and John Quincy Adams had enthralled their hearers.

In each presidential election year, small ragamuffin armies appeared bearing banners with strange devices—Greenbackers and National Laborites, Anti-Monopolists and Prohibitionists. Their votes were numbered in the thousands against Democratic and Republican millions; their enthusiastic slogans were drowned out in the hoarse cheering of major party torchlight parades. The fringe parties scarcely seemed to disturb the political pattern that had been created 20 years after Appomattox. Yet clearly, by 1888, the stage was set for a sharp challenge to the whole system of spoils, congressional supremacy and benign federal support of vested interests. In the 1890s, under the impetus of a great depression, volcanic upheavals would shatter the old forms. The ideas of the third parties, if not the parties themselves, would have their day. But the time was not quite ripe.

Frances Folsom was the daughter of an old friend of Grover Cleveland. When Frances' father died, Cleveland took care of her and her mother, and it was rumored that he had designs on Mrs. Folsom. He grumbled that ". . . the papers keep marrying me to old ladies. . . ." and married Frances.

Inside the cartoon:

THE $OLID $OUTH MUST BE WATCHED OR THEY WILL PREY

REFORM IS NECESSARY AND WE MUST WATCH THAT IT IS CARRIED OUT IN GOOD FAITH.

"The Democratic plan of counting the vote seems to have been this: Don't wait for any returns, but manufacture figures enough to establish a plausible claim. Then, if the actual returns don't agree with the figures, a basis is secured upon which to shout 'fraud.' Then yell 'fraud' till the last minute." —N.Y.Tribune.

READY FOR BATTLE, Thomas Nast shows himself sharpening a pro-Hayes pencil for the 1876 election. When the disputed votes forced Hayes to bargain with the South in order to win, Nast balked. Silenced by his editor, he later drew himself being choked.

A master of pictorial politics

A SELF-STYLED "little fat Dutch boy" stood tall on the political horizons of late 19th Century America. Presidents courted his good will, and evil men quivered under his lash. His views of affairs were sometimes sentimental, often witty, but always brimful of loathing for corruption and thunderous in calling for righteousness. More to the point, his opinions could swing elections. This powerful man was German-born Thomas Nast (*above*), for 24 years chief political cartoonist for *Harper's Weekly*. Lincoln, praising Nast's Civil War pictures, called him the Union's "best recruiting sergeant." Grant believed he owed his election to the presidency to Sheridan's sword and Nast's pencil. Three others could attribute their political fortunes to Nast: Hayes and Cleveland, both elected President with his help, and Tammany Hall's Boss Tweed, sent to jail after a long Nast campaign.

Nast had the nation's eye. *Harper's* considered his cartoons worth 200,000 subscriptions. He was not only the greatest American cartoonist of his time but the first to become a public figure in his own right. Although there had been political cartoons in America for a century, Nast virtually invented cartooning as a profession. And the creatures he shaped on his drawing board, from Tammany tiger to Uncle Sam, are still the common coin of cartooning.

"LET US PREY" prays Boss Tweed, chief of the Tammany Hall boodlers. Nast has drawn them here as vultures trying to wait out the storm he has raised up against them.

"'TWAS HIM" says the Tammany Ring to the query, "Who stole the people's money?" These jabs so worried Tweed (*left*) that Nast was offered $500,000 to go off to Europe. "My constituents can't read; but, damn it, they can see pictures!" exploded Bill Tweed.

TAMMANY'S TIGER, fierce and rapacious, glowers (*below*) from *Harper's Weekly* two days before the election of 1871. The caption quoted Tweed's question: "What are you going to do about it?" The city, to Thomas Nast's delight, defeated Tammany.

A war waged in ink against Tammany and Tweedism

WHEN little Tommy Nast was growing up in New York, he would cheer as the Americus Fire Company, with Foreman Bill Tweed racing at its head, charged by his house. The boy Nast loved the tiger his heroes had painted on their engine. It was, he thought, the fiercest, finest tiger ever. And, dreaming of old masters, he sometimes doodled tigers in his schoolbooks.

Bill Tweed, too, dreamed, but of another old master—Samuel Swartwout, who stole a million dollars in government money and got clean away to Europe in 1837.

This impressed Tweed, for Sam's name came to be used as a verb; "to swartwout" meant to defraud grandly. And Big Bill, once he became Grand Sachem of Tammany Hall and boss of New York City, knew how to swartwout. He paid a carpenter $360,747.61 for a month's work and a plasterer $2,870,464.06 for nine months; most of this found its way back into the pockets of Tweed and his friends. In all he took the town for $200 million, while Nast, who had turned the Americus tiger into the beast of Tammany, thundered against him.

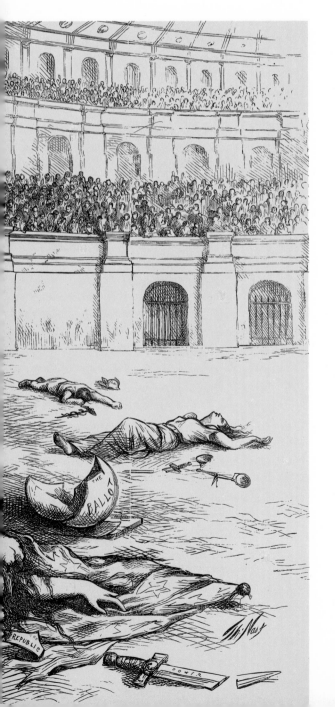

TWEED'S CAPTURE was brought about by this Nast cartoon: Spanish police used it to identify the fleeing Tammany leader when he arrived at Vigo disguised as a sailor. Tweed died in a New York jail.

In a Nast cartoon fighting inflationary ideas during the 1873 panic, Uncle Sam laughs at money bag that huffs and puffs to blow itself up.

A zooful of Nast's political fantasies

UNCLE SAM, that symbolic American, existed before Nast came along, but as a country bumpkin sometimes called Brother Jonathan. Nast spruced him up and turned him into today's stern but kindly father figure. All the other now familiar cartoon devices on these pages—the inflationary windbag, Republican elephant and the Democratic donkey—were invented by the man who signed himself Th. Nast.

Nast had his prickly side. He believed firmly that his pictures should reflect his opinions and not those of George William Curtis, the editor of *Harper's Weekly*. As a result the magazine sometimes ran cartoons that laughed away the very issues (such as whether Nast's friend Grant was trying to play Caesar) that Curtis took seriously. Curtis could not even protest in person, for Nast, an urbane little man who was a favorite companion of Mark Twain and Edwin Booth, was never in the office long enough to listen to the editor's complaints.

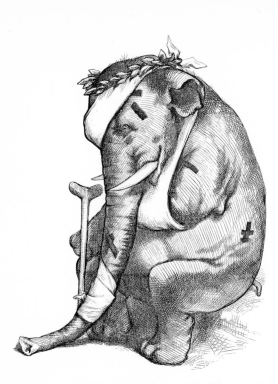

THE REPUBLICAN ELEPHANT, first used by Nast to show big votes, rests after the close Hayes-Tilden election of 1876 and quotes King Pyrrhus: "Another such victory and I am undone."

THE DEMOCRATIC DONKEY is urged by Senator Thomas F. Bayard to scramble back on "The Safe and Sound Financial Road" to the presidency. "Hold on," Bayard cries as he himself digs his heels in, "and you may walk over the sluggish animal up there yet."

TIGER AND LAMB lie down together in a cartoon showing Nast's growing distrust over Republican Hayes's policy of trying to appease the Democratic South. That the lamb lies inside the Democratic tiger is a matter that slowly dawns on the viewer.

23

THE CAMPAIGNING REPUBLICANS of 1876 are shown tramping on a two-headed Democratic tiger. The tiger's body links the "hard money" policies of presidential candidate Samuel J. Tilden (at right) with the "soft money" policies of the vice-presidential candidate, Thomas A. Hendricks (at left). The man with empty pockets is John Kelly, Tweed's successor.

The battles for sound money

THE financial panic of 1873 touched off demands that the government loosen credit by issuing more paper money, or greenbacks. This split the major parties into "soft" and "hard" money factions, and a third party, the Greenback, arose to fight for inflation. Tom Nast flailed away at the "soft money" forces with vigorous cartoons like the ones on these pages. One of his targets, John Logan of Illinois, growled: "Little Nast thinks he can teach statesmen how to run the government. Anybody might think he runs it himself." Nast retorted that the inflationists were "peevish schoolboys, worthless of such honor"—that is, of being drawn by Thomas Nast.

FIGHTING INFLATION, Nast shows the Massachusetts politician Ben Butler caring for the inflationary Rag Baby. Butler won elections as a Republican, a Greenback and a Democrat.

CROWNING AN HEIR, Peter Cooper, millionaire, philanthropist, inventor and 1876 Greenback candidate for the presidency, invests Ben Butler as his successor in 1884 —using the inflated cushion Cooper always took with him to ease the pain of hard seats.

25

The closing campaigns
of an indomitable fighter

AT his peak Thomas Nast earned $25,000 a year, lived expansively—and was politically restless. He was wrathy at Hayes in 1877, disgusted with James Garfield in 1880 and finally so appalled by James G. Blaine in 1884 *(opposite)* that he supported the Democrat Cleveland. So did *Harper's Weekly*. But it had pointed out in 1880 that its editorial policy was to be found in its editorials, not its cartoons. The warmth between magazine and cartoonist slowly cooled, and in 1888 they parted.

After that, Nast seemed to lose his touch. It became increasingly hard to find markets for his cartoons. He lost money in investments. He was in need in 1902 when President Theodore Roosevelt named him to a $4,000-a-year job as consul in far-off Guayaquil, Ecuador. From there Nast wrote to his family that yellow fever was rampant in the town. It claimed a man at his club, another at his boardinghouse. "It is," he wrote, "coming very near." And just four and a half months after he took over his new position, Thomas Nast, aged 62, was dead of it.

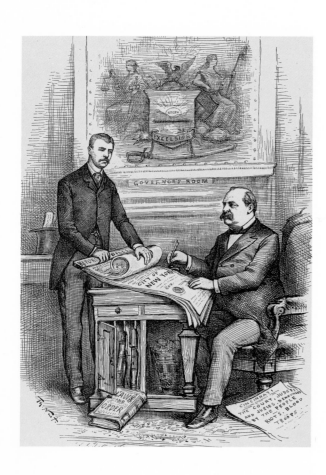

RISING POLITICIANS, New York's Democratic Governor Grover Cleveland and Republican Assemblyman Theodore Roosevelt, two Nast favorites *(left)*, appear in an 1884 cartoon. Cleveland is signing reform bills that Roosevelt had introduced in the legislature.

EAGER CANDIDATE James G. Blaine is attacked as a phony "plumed knight" riding in a jousting match for the public's money. Grover Cleveland won the election, but Nast and *Harper's Weekly* never quite recovered from their change-over in parties.

2. THE IMPACT OF INDUSTRIAL GROWTH

IN the quarter century of mechanical marvels that followed the political Compromise of 1877 the American people rushed pell-mell into the complexity of modern civilization. Within a generation they developed the world's greatest industrial economy—complete with troubles, triumphs, victims and victors. Flinging themselves upon the virgin resources of the continent, they mobilized armies of workers, organized arsenals of new machinery, tapped reservoirs of capital and created hitherto undreamed-of products. On a new and grandiose scale, they encountered every reward and problem of greatness.

In the process, Americans came to discover a painful paradox of progress. Their prodigious achievements had been largely the product of a social and political system which gave a maximum of equality, mobility and opportunity to all men. Yet in a huge, complex and maturing industrial order it was increasingly difficult to preserve these virtues. By the end of the century, the public was beginning to reshape its historic views of the "American" significance of such terms as freedom, individualism, progress, morality.

The grand Centennial Exposition of 1876 in Philadelphia afforded an amazing preview of the changes to come. The crowds that flocked to it got their money's worth in wonders. They gaped at the exotic Japanese exhibit, the Italian statuary, the fountain of French cologne. There were also things of much greater substance and import: gear-cutting machines, hydraulic pumps, towering steam engines, and remarkable new farm implements. Industry was

ASSASSINATED PRESIDENT James A. Garfield is seen in a memorial portrait painted after his death. In his few months in office he began reforming the postal service.

exalted, and Walt Whitman urged the Muse of Poetry to "migrate from Greece" to take her rightful place amid the new achievements of vigorous America, "bluff'd not a bit by drainpipe, gasometers, artificial fertilizers."

American industry could certainly have used a muse with a proper gift for epic and a lively sense of humor. Already growing briskly by 1876, the story of the growth of industry in the next 30 years would be a saga of sweat, ambition and avarice, with a significance far surpassing even its staggering statistics. American ability to produce machine-made goods and distribute them nationally increased in spectacular fashion. From 1860 to 1890, the value of manufactures soared from less than two billion to over nine billion dollars.

Out of this mushrooming rose new cities and men. The cities needed luck or location to become industrial centers. The men needed luck or cunning or driving strength or inventive skill—the formula varied—to succeed. Some swept to power on a tide of profits, but many unlucky ones drowned.

The leading industries in the expansion were rails, steel, petroleum products, processed foods, fuels, metals and communications. When examined, all show a similar interplay of factors: abundant resources, improved transportation leading to a continent-wide market, a favorable social and legal climate, technological breakthroughs and entrepreneurial boldness.

FIRST came the railroads, rushing to meet the challenge of a continent that needed to be knit together. The earliest transcontinental line was completed in 1869, covering the 1,800 miles of prairie, desert and mountain between Omaha and Sacramento. The western section was the task of the Central Pacific Railroad Company, the creature of four men—Leland Stanford, Charles Crocker, Collis P. Huntington and Mark Hopkins. Sacramento grocery and hardware merchants, they had started with the relatively modest ambition of monopolizing the trade of the mining camps. Then an engineering genius, Theodore Judah, sold them on the idea of a transcontinental line; Washington obligingly gave them 10 to 20 square miles of public land plus loans of up to $48,000 for every mile they could finish.

With these advances as a base, the ingenious promoters were able through complicated financing schemes to reduce their personal investments to a minimum while retaining control of immensely profitable properties. From 1863 on, armies of imported Chinese coolies laid track, sweating in Nevada's alkali dust or chipping roadbeds into the sides of mile-high Sierra cliffs. Starting from Omaha, the Union Pacific Company, similarly endowed by the government, sent its engineers, Irish laborers, teamsters and commissary agents westward across the plains. The two lines came together at Promontory, Utah, in May of 1869, amid oratory and the popping of champagne corks.

But it was obvious to thoughtful men that the great West would require more than a single line to deliver its wealth. The Atchison, Topeka and Santa Fe was largely the child of a Pennsylvania lawyer, Cyrus K. Holliday, who went to Kansas in the '50s. In 1863 he helped talk Congress into offering a huge land grant for a railroad to link the Missouri Valley with Santa Fe in the territory of New Mexico. His railroad would take the romance out of the old Santa Fe trail, true. But Holliday had romantic visions of his own. A bare seven miles were laid when he led an excursion out along the tracks, struck an attitude and announced that the road would some day reach not only Santa Fe but Chicago, St. Louis, Galveston, Mexico City and San Francisco.

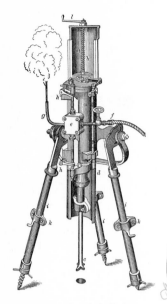

The Ingersoll rock drill, first automatic machine of its kind, was a great spur to the booming construction business of the late 19th Century. Although it made millions, inventor Simon Ingersoll took only $50 for the design, sold all rights to the tool for a nominal sum and died nearly penniless.

The band saw, designed about 1815, for many years had little use because of breakage of the delicate blades. When stronger blades were developed late in the century, artisans ran riot creating the gingerbread scrollwork for Victorian extravaganzas which were nicknamed "Carpenter Renaissance."

By 1872 his road had reached the Colorado boundary. The first purchase order—30,000 tons of iron rail at $100 a ton—showed the immensity of the problems Holliday faced. Whenever he could get enough credit to procure material, his work gangs would struggle onward against unique obstacles. Cheyenne and Arapaho braves looked disdainfully on the toiling palefaces and raided supply dumps; grasshoppers died on the tracks in such numbers that work trains stalled in a slime of crushed green bodies. No wonder that on Saturday night the men rushed to spend their two-dollar-a-day earnings in the shantytowns and saloons that sprang up behind them. Nor that the local paper could announce when Pueblo, Colorado, was reached in 1876: "The biggest drunk of the present century will occur here on the 7th of March."

In 1880 the line did reach Santa Fe. Already it was branching out, fighting rival roads for the Colorado silver trade. Directors and lawyers battled in court; work gangs with guns sometimes moved in to grab a key mountain pass from a rival line's construction crews. By 1883 the Santa Fe—as the road would always be known—was in California, fighting the Southern Pacific (owned by the same "Big Four" who had built the Central Pacific from California to Utah) with injunction, purchase and incorporation as well as with fists and deadly spike hammers. Thus the nation got another transcontinental line.

The Southern Pacific itself finished a connection to New Orleans in 1883. The same year saw the end of a long process of railroad building in Minnesota, Dakota and Montana when the Northern Pacific—also provided with a land bounty—joined the line of the Oregon Railway and Navigation Company, which ran to the Pacific, near Helena. Ten years later a veteran of the river-boat trade, James J. Hill, had the satisfaction of completing the Great Northern, which linked St. Paul and Seattle.

Hill was an unusual promoter in an era which saw most railway directors encourage rapid and shoddy construction to qualify for land grants and government subsidies, or milk the stockholder through dummy construction companies owned by the directors and officers. Hill's Great Northern, completed without subsidy, was carefully built, and it was tireless in its efforts to attract substantial immigrants and improve farm practices in the Northwest.

THE nation had five transcontinental trunk lines by 1893, and national mileage leaped from some 35,000 to nearly 260,000 between 1865 and 1900. In the East railroad construction went on at a brisk clip. New England trackage merely doubled in the 50 years after 1860, but the Middle Atlantic states quadrupled their mileage; the mileage in the Old Northwest (Indiana, Illinois, Ohio, Michigan and Wisconsin) rose from under 10,000 to 45,000; the states of the Confederacy increased their 1860 totals more than sevenfold, to 63,000. In 1887 the work gangs spiked down a record 12,878 miles. The roads not only grew bigger, but better and safer. By the 1890s gauges and time zones had been standardized, air brakes and automatic couplers installed, locomotives improved, rails strengthened, and Pullman and dining cars added. Train travel was fast leaving behind the time when a journey was a flirtation with dyspepsia, freezing, suffocation and injury.

Railroad building in the East and Midwest lacked the romance and danger of the transcontinentals. But there was solid economic significance to the work of the dozens of feeder lines that crisscrossed every state. By integrating the total national production effort in a hundred different ways, the

Looking like a fugitive from a carrousel, this steam engine for street railways was so contrived to avoid frightening horses. The inventor claimed that its cost would be only one dollar per 15 hours. An added feature was that it could stop within 20 feet, even at the fantastic speed of eight miles an hour.

During the 1880s and '90s, inventors brought forth innumerable wheeled contraptions. The Pedespeed (above) seemed to have obvious social advantages, but it had competition from devices like the bicycle skate, a two-wheeled gadget similar to the Pedespeed, and the Decemtuple, a bicycle for 10.

railroads were doing more than any imaginable political arrangement to make the country a single trade area. It was a new America in which Minnesota flour and Iowa lard went into pies baked in Ohio-made ovens by Vermont matrons; in which Wisconsin farmers pulled on Massachusetts boots and turned their Chicago harvesters into the north forty.

Private investors had supposedly put nearly $10 billion into the American railroad system by 1900, though part of this figure represented watered stock. To it must be added some 180 million acres of land given the roads by state and national governments, plus loans of $65 million by the federal government alone. Much of the money lined the pockets of railroad builders like Jay Gould, the upstate New York grocery clerk turned foxy stock market operator, who squeezed out of such roads as the Erie, Union Pacific and others a fortune estimated at $77 million. But the railroads also fulfilled a great need and it is not easy to say that the nation failed to get value for its investment.

Rails represented one index of the growth of a modern industrial economy. Steel was another. Here, too, technological innovation, furious energy and deft promotion united in a spectacular boom. In 1867, when fewer than 20,000 tons were turned out, steel scarcely counted in the American economy. The techniques for mass production were already in existence; in the 1850s American ironmaster William Kelly and British inventor Henry Bessemer had both

TRANSCONTINENTALS
BRIDGE THE NATION

Five great railroads spanned the U.S. by 1893, opening new land to settlers and carrying eastward the riches of the West. The Union Pacific was the first to be completed; in 1869 work crews met at Promontory, Utah. (The date and place of other join-ups are shown on map.) Western cities grew: Omaha, from 16,000 to 140,000; Salt Lake City from 13,000 to 45,000; Seattle, from 2,000 to 40,000. Elsewhere, Canada pushed a line to the Pacific Coast. Russia extended track across Siberia; France dug the Suez Canal. By water and rail the world was newly knit together.

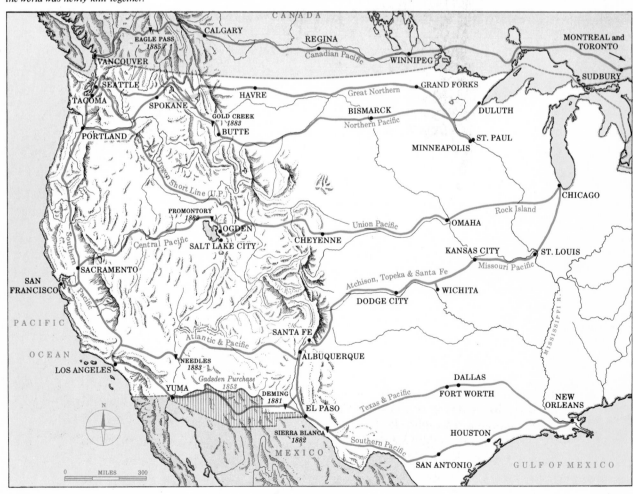

patented processes for burning the impurities out of molten iron by forcing a draft of air through it.

By the middle of the Civil War, small beginnings had been made toward "Bessemerizing" the substantial iron industry. There would be later and better methods, but Bessemer's process offered the quickest, cheapest way to make a steel tough and strong enough for the railroads, the major potential customers. Bessemer steel was a vast improvement over wrought iron; the country produced far more of it than any other kind until the 20th Century. One of the early "Steel Kings" was Eber Ward, called "Captain" because he had risen from cabin boy to ownership of a fleet of Great Lakes steamships. Later, he converted his holdings to furnaces and rolling mills, and began making steel near Detroit in 1864, using Kelly's patents. Alexander Holley, a mechanical engineer who specialized in locomotive design, got the American rights to Bessemer's process at about this time and, after a brisk patent fight with Ward, drew the captain into a merger in which Holley had the upper hand.

Enlisting partners, Holley built steel plants at such diverse points as St. Louis, Chicago, Pittsburgh, Harrisburg, and Troy, New York. These he visited regularly, improving and correcting as he went. Men like Ward and Holley pushed production of Bessemer steel to 335,283 tons by 1875 and lowered its price to secure quantity orders by railroads.

Leland Stanford was vain and wealthy. As president of the Central Pacific Railroad he ordered his employees to salute as he rode by in his private car, straightforwardly named "The Stanford." He loved mechanical toys; in his home was a flock of metal birds which opened their tin beaks and sang.

BY then, Andrew Carnegie was entering the field. He did not create the railroad-building era which opened a profitable market for steel for a generation, nor the Sault Ste. Marie canal, which made it feasible to exploit the vast iron ore deposits around Lake Superior. These forces made the steel boom. But Carnegie saw the opportunities, and he seized them to become the greatest American steelmaker. He nursed the industry by his foresight, fed it with investments and built a popular industrial philosophy on it.

He was an orthodox rags-to-riches hero. In 1848, aged 12, he came to America with his father, a poor Scottish weaver. His first job, in a Pennsylvania cotton mill, paid $1.20 a week. At 18 he attracted the notice of the Pennsylvania Railroad's Tom Scott and became that railroad baron's secretary and telegraph operator. He was earning only $420 a year, but was already looking for investment opportunities. Carnegie meant it when he later told young men that "if any of you have saved as much as $50 or $100 I do not know any branch of business into which you cannot plunge at once."

More and more he concentrated on fabricators of heavy-duty iron products. While still with the Pennsylvania, he organized his own company to make railroad bridges and sold much of its stock to his employer. By 1865, when he left the Pennsylvania, he was collecting thousands in annual dividends. His continuing close ties to the railroad earned him a chance to sell six million dollars worth of the Pennsylvania's bonds in 1872 at a lavish commission.

Convinced that steel, rather than iron, was the metal of the future, Carnegie built a Bessemer plant near Pittsburgh. He hired a production genius named William Jones, a burly Union veteran who tackled technical problems with impetuous zest. Jones drove and hustled Carnegie's workmen. Roaring through the plant, making innovations on the spot, firing and rehiring men as fast as a hot Welsh temper allowed and ultimately drawing $50,000 a year (as much as the President of the United States then made), Jones was a production man who died with his boots on in 1889 in a blast furnace accident.

Carnegie was not only a builder of a steel empire, but also an inspired sales-man of capitalism, of "triumphant democracy" as he called it. Without benefit of public relations experts, he dashed off articles praising philanthropy, com-petition, and the rights and duties of wealth. "All hail, King Steel," he wrote in 1901, "and success to the republic, the future seat and centre of his empire, where he is to sit enthroned and work his wonders upon the earth."

By then, Carnegie had built up an integrated steel empire which included railroads, mines, ore boats and the vast coke ovens of his longtime associate Henry Clay Frick, another self-made man. The weaver's boy was ready to sell out to J. P. Morgan for nearly half a billion dollars, and spend his last 18 years in travel and fantastic feats of philanthropy. And by then the United States could produce in a year over 12 million tons of steel to eight million for Germany, its nearest rival. What was more, America could produce it at $15 per ton, according to Carnegie. This was two-thirds of one cent for one pound of steel—into which went "two pounds of iron ore mined and transported by rail and water 1,000 miles, one pound of coke, requiring one and one-third pounds of coal to be mined, coked, and transported 50 miles, and one-third of a pound of limestone quarried and transported 140 miles."

What this transformation meant is perhaps suggested best by two accounts of Pittsburgh. In 1802 a French traveler described it as a town of "not more than 40 or 50 acres in extent," housing its people in 400 widely separated brick homes. In 1890, a delegation of British ironmakers reported that Pitts-burgh used 750 million feet of natural gas a day. It had 21 blast furnaces, 49 iron foundries, 15,000 coke ovens and 33 rolling mills. Pittsburgh had become the city of smoke and steel, its skies reddened by blast furnace fires at night.

Henry Clay Frick was a million-aire by the time he was 30. Frail as a youth, he was no weakling with his employees. In the 1892 strike at Homestead, he tried to bring armed guards to the plant and set off a battle. The strike, dur-ing which Frick himself was shot and stabbed, destroyed the union.

W HEREVER one looked, the same combination of God's bounty and man's driving cleverness seemed to be making America over into a nation of men who could not produce wealth fast enough. In 1859, for example, oil was discovered in the northwest corner of Pennsylvania simultaneously with the perfection of practical methods for distilling raw petroleum into kerosene for lamps. Within 10 years the area boasted a boom as gaudy and full of shoot-ing, thieving, drinking and wenching as anything in the Wild West.

A young Cleveland produce merchant named John D. Rockefeller looked the place over and concluded that while the refining of crude oil was waste-fully and incompetently carried on, it had possibilities. During the Civil War he invested $4,000 in a small refinery. In less than 20 years his Standard Oil Company controlled over 90 per cent of the refining industry, then processing more than 28 million barrels annually. (Standard Oil never quite achieved the complete monopoly legend credits it with.) Oil lamps were being replaced by the electric light, invented by Thomas A. Edison in 1879, but the newly de-veloped internal combustion engine held out long-term prospects to refiners.

John Pierpont Morgan admired beautiful women and handsome men. He lavished attention on the women and preferred good-looking business associates. A domineer-ing man, he met his match in Theo-dore Roosevelt. When Teddy left for Africa, Morgan hoped that "the first lion he meets does his duty."

In meat packing, the pace was equally hectic. A Scottish traveler in Chica-go described an 1868 visit to a very modern slaughterhouse. A line of pigs was marched in. Each pig "was clutched by the snout; stuck; run by machinery up to the top of the building; plunged into a long tank of hot water; shot from hand to hand and scraped; hooked up and run on by machinery, ripped down, cut into parts, dressed and salted. . . . Within twelve minutes from the time when it was an intelligent pig on the gangway [, it was] converted into pork, packed in barrels, and ready for shipment."

The great railroad expansion of the 1870s which brought the livestock to Chicago, and the successful use of refrigerator cars from 1875 on, converted slaughtering from a local to a national business. A new breed of immensely wealthy packers, headed by such men as Philip Armour, Nelson Morris and Gustavus Swift, emerged in Kansas City and Chicago. As a consequence, most of the hitherto important local slaughterers went under in competition with the Western packers. In 1870 the dollar value of meat packed in the United States was under $65 million; by 1890 it was above half a billion dollars.

JUST as railroads and machines vastly increased the amount of meat prepared for 19th Century tables, so did they furnish, in conjunction with virgin soils, an abundance of bread. In 1860 Minneapolis and St. Paul between them had some 16,000 inhabitants. Then a canny Maine businessman, Cadwallader C. Washburn, came there with a faith that the hard spring wheat of the northern plains could somehow become pure white flour. Previously, millers had been able to get only a coarse, brownish meal from it. Washburn and his partners introduced a French invention, the middlings-purifier, which helped solve the problem. A rival miller, Charles A. Pillsbury, installed an improved system of grinding (also borrowed from Europe) which, by passing the wheat through a series of chilled steel rollers, avoided discoloration of the flour while preserving the gluten content of the wheat.

As railroads reached out into the Dakotas, the Minneapolis millers harnessed the fall of the Mississippi to their mill wheels and bought Number One Hard wheat by the carload. In 1886 the city's great flour mills were handling 35 million bushels a year and their daily output of flour filled 328 railroad cars. The little twin towns on the river had become the grinding capital of the world.

The men, like David A. Wells, who hymned these productive marvels, gleefully ran statistics through their fingers, held them up to the light, hugged them. In 1885 a newly invented glass-melting furnace, Wells noted, let four men produce a million square feet of glass a month; before, 28 men needed a month to produce 115,000 square feet. In 1840 a worker in a cotton mill, putting in a 14-hour day, turned out 9,600 yards of sheeting; in 1886 he could produce 30,000 yards in a mere 10-hour day. In agriculture, David Wells joyously reported that a variety of new machines had "combined to make the change in farm-work almost a revolution."

Communications kept pace. The Western Union Company operated 400,-000 miles of wire in 1883—and the telegraph was only 39 years old. The telephone was invented in 1875; by 1900 there were 1,356,000 in the nation. Both instruments knit together the growing cities, which in turn showed a voracious appetite for many other products. Introduction of electric street lamps in 1879 and electric street railways in 1888 started a complete new industry of electric generators and motors. Electrified transit systems, like the great new bridges, demanded steel. New York City installed its first elevated train in 1870, finished the Brooklyn Bridge in 1883 and added the Williamsburg span by 1903. In 1885 Chicago built a metal-framed building, 10 stories high —and by the end of the century the skyscraper loomed as one possible kind of architectural monument that an industrial civilization could originate.

Individual statistics cannot truly catch the spirit of this sweating, shoving, lusty last quarter of the century. A few key figures do vaguely outline the

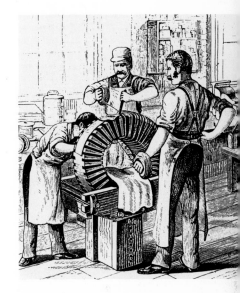

In a factory of the 1880s, workmen wind the armature for a piece of heavy-duty electrical machinery. The light and power industry was still young, but toward the end of the century the first street lights began to brighten cities, and straphangers fought over seats on the newfangled electric trolley cars.

picture of what had been an agrarian republic turning into a country of "rivet and girder, motor and dynamo . . . steel-faced cities, reaching at the skies." The 1860 census found over six million "gainful workers" in agriculture, fewer than two million in manufacturing and construction; some four million in all nonfarming occupations combined. By 1880, farmers totaled slightly less than the 8,780,000 nonfarm workers. By 1900, the not quite 11 million farm workers were far outweighed by the 18 million who worked elsewhere.

More significant to show how rapidly America was moving from countryside to city are these figures: In 1860 people living in towns and cities with more than 2,500 residents, totaled six million out of 30 million. By 1880, some 14 million lived in such nonrural places as against 36 million who did not. In 1900, the ratio was about 30 million to 46 million. Between 1880 and 1900, the number of places with populations of 5,000 to 10,000 jumped from 249 to 465, places with 10,000 to 25,000 from 146 to 280, those between 100,000 and 250,000 from 12 to 23, and those above a quarter million from four to nine.

In 1889 David Wells, that indefatigable eulogist of his period, listed items "which in their understanding, possession, and common use the world now regards as constituting the dividing lines between civilization and barbarism." All had been invented within the preceding 50 years. They included mechanical reapers, the Bessemer process, the telegraph, photography, the industrial use of rubber, the sewing machine, the electric motor and light, guncotton and dynamite, the rotary printing press—and Wells wound up a marathon sentence with a final breathless, unorganized burst: "iron and steel ships, pressed glass, wire rope, petroleum and its derivatives, and aniline dyes; the industrial use of the metal nickel, cottonseed oil, artificial butter, stearine-candles, natural gas, cheap postage, and the postage stamp." If the list ended in something of an anticlimax, Wells nevertheless had no doubt that its significance would correspond in importance with achievements of the past, including "the invention of gunpowder, the emancipation of thought through the Reformation, and the invention of the steam-engine; when the whole plane of civilization and humanity rose to a higher level."

In the long run, perhaps, that lack of doubt was the most important thing about the 25 years which began in the centennial summer of 1876. Americans—and Western Europeans, on the whole—were unshaken in their belief that the power to mass-produce goods and transport them with incredible cheapness could be a force only for good. "Work has sometimes been called worship," wrote an author named Franklin Wilson in a little treatise of 1874 entitled *Wealth; Its Acquisition, Investment and Use,* "and the dusty, smoky workshop a temple; because there man glorifies the great Architect by imitating him in providing for the wants of his creatures."

The "workman" whom Wilson and his age delighted to honor was not the operative who stood at the machine, but the daring entrepreneur who had furnished the capital for the machine. Around him all the glories of production shone. A delegate to a laboring men's convention in 1874 might insist that "the wealth producers of this nation are the men and women who dig, delve, and spin." The prestige, however, as well as the cash, went to those who saved their money and organized the digging and delving of others—and the emerging tycoons conspicuously lacked humility.

"Those who are most successful in the acquisition of property," said Andrew

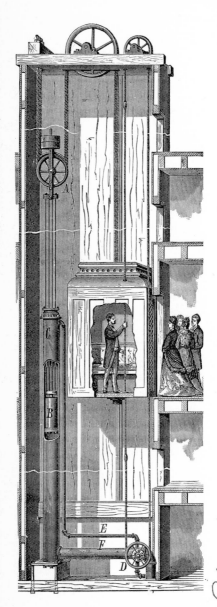

W. E. Hale installed the first lift in the Capitol in Washington. An earlier model, the Duplex Water Elevator, was operated by a piston pushed by a column of water. The mechanism was so simple and had so few moving parts to create friction that Hale said proudly, "It should . . . last until worn out."

Carnegie with great unction, "and who acquire it to such an enormous extent are the very men who are able to control it, to invest it, and to handle it in the way most useful to society." Some of the craftsmen displaced by all this miraculous machinery grumbled darkly that "in the present arrangement of labor and capital the condition of the employee is simply that of wage slavery." Yet Russell Conwell, the first president of Temple University, shouted to youthful audiences: "I say that you ought to get rich, and it is your duty to get rich. . . . To make money honestly is to preach the gospel."

Lillian Sholes, probably the first woman typist, sits at her father's machine. Although about 50 designs preceded Sholes's, his was the first marketed and his keyboard remains almost unchanged. "I feel," Sholes wrote, "that I have done something for the women who have always had to work so hard."

IT was not so strange, after all, that Rockefellers and Carnegies seemed more powerful, attractive and worthy of emulation than the "statesmen" playing musical chairs in politics. The country longed to believe in full the businessmen's own all too smug assertions that power, daring and imagination were glorified in the life of trade as it was carried on in the modern world. American expansiveness, optimism, and passion for speed and growth fed on the mounting sales and export totals, and on the visible cheapening in cost of the necessary things of life and innumerable other goods. Drawbacks, doubts and hesitations brought on by business setbacks were swept aside by the enthusiasm of a young giant for new playthings. In this euphoric atmosphere, little attention was paid to the few skeptical dissenters like Henry Adams, who appraised the American of 1892 as a man who "had no sense of relative values, and knew not what to do with his money when he got it except use it to make more, or throw it away."

Perhaps the national mood had been most vividly captured in the satirical novel of 1873, *The Gilded Age*. There Mark Twain and Charles Dudley Warner had created the unforgettable character of "Colonel" Beriah Sellers, a seedy but magnificently undismayable promoter whose head teemed with get-rich-quick schemes. One of them, he explained to a young friend, was to be the manufacture of "Beriah Sellers' infallible Imperial Oriental Optic Liniment and Salvation for Sore Eyes—the Medical Wonder of the Age! Small bottles, 50 cents, large ones a dollar. Average cost, five and seven cents for the two sizes." The first year, the Colonel explained, warming up as he improvised, sales might be 55,000 bottles.

> The second year, sales would reach 200,000 bottles—clear profit, say, $75,000—and in the meantime the great factory would be building in St. Louis to cost, say, $100,000. The third year we could easily sell one million bottles in the United States . . . profit at least $350,000—and then it would begin to be time to turn our attention toward the real idea of the business. . . . Three years of introductory trade in the Orient and what will be the result? Why, our headquarters would be in Constantinople and our hindquarters in Further India! Factories and warehouses in Cairo, Ispahan, Bagdad, Damascus, Jerusalem, Yedo, Peking, Bangkok, Delhi, Bombay, and Calcutta! Annual income—well, God only knows how many millions and millions apiece!

America was full of Beriah Sellerses in the 1870s. The incredible thing was that 20 to 30 years later, the dreams of some of them had come true. America had generated Sellers and his kind in a century of independence, but never really thought of what would happen if their feverish visions became reality, or their ambitions were transmuted into genuine power. The search for an answer to that question was the post-Civil War generation's main task.

The amazing men of many marvels

WIZARDS walked the world in the magical later years of the 19th Century, or so it seemed. They set the gloom of night aglow with cheery electric light, enabled the people in all corners of the land to talk to one another. They made machines that talked, cameras a child could work, typewriters, barbed wire and workable safety pins. As they produced their marvels the soldiers and statesmen, the nation's heroes for two thirds of the century, faded away. Now the heroes were the inventors—Thomas Alva Edison, Alexander Graham Bell, John Augustus Roebling, George Eastman, George Westinghouse. These men and others like them were all busy creating new industries, new jobs, new wealth. (Total national income quadrupled between 1869 and 1901.) They built a new civilization, based on machines and mass production. Later it would be argued that they were not true pioneers in science, but only super-talented mechanics. But America brushed such talk aside, and the first official act of Mark Twain's Connecticut Yankee after taking over the Wizard Merlin's post at King Arthur's court was to set up a patent office, for "a country without a patent office and good patent laws," he wrote, "was just a crab, and couldn't travel any way but sideways or backways."

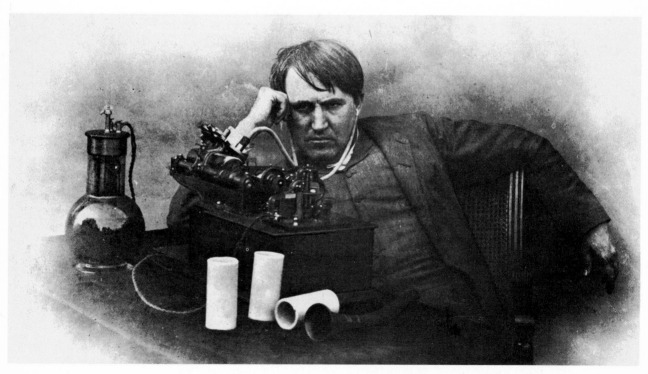

GRIMLY VICTORIOUS, Thomas A. Edison listens to his talking machine at 5 a.m. on June 16, 1888. To beat rivals, he had just perfected it after 72 hours of driving, sleepless work.

A GROWING MAZE of wires enshrouds New York. The danger inherent in these electric webs became apparent when they fell during the blizzard of 1888. They were then forced underground.

Ohio's bumptious son and his incandescent light

From the invention of the phonograph on, Tom Edison was the arrogant central figure of the 19th Century's age of invention. People watched him with fascination inspired by a master magician and showman; newspapers speculated on what new wonder he would bring forth next. When Edison announced he expected to invent the electric light in six weeks, stock exchanges quivered and gas-company shares crashed. The English Parliament declared he could not do it and, of course, he did not. It took a little more than a year.

A fanciful painting shows Edison's Menlo Park laboratories, over which floats the electric light, invented there in 1879. At the far right is

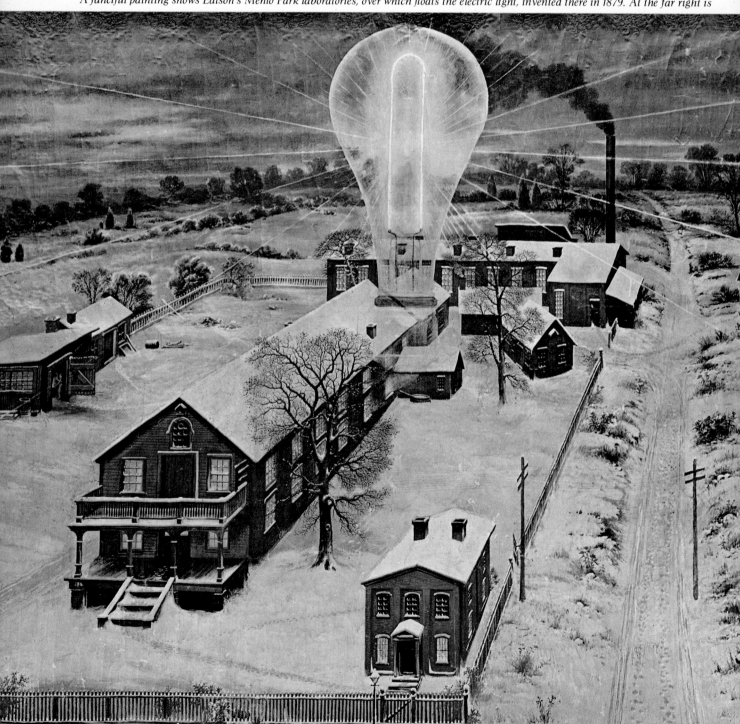

Tom Edison stocked the world with much of its modern furniture. He improved telephones and telegraphs, made electric motors that could move elevators and trains, designed motion-picture cameras and projectors. He noted the movement of electrons in vacuums, the "Edison effect," that led to radio tubes. And always he remained stubbornly at odds with pure science. Speaking of his studious son Theodore, he sighed and said, "His forte is mathematics. I am a little afraid . . . he may go flying off into the clouds with that fellow Einstein."

A LOVELY HORN, like a morning-glory in full bloom, marks this 1908 Edison phonograph.

an electric train which Edison built early in 1880.

A DEDICATED CREW, Edison and his aides pose stiffly under the electric lights in the workroom at Menlo Park. Here they toiled long hours, sometimes to music from the organ at the rear. At other times Edison would take them fishing.

"THE BLACK MARIA," the first movie studio *(above)*, attracts visitors at Edison's West Orange laboratories. The building was mounted on a turntable so that its open roof could always be pointed at the sun, essential for primitive cameras.

41

Boston's ingenious Scot and his wonderful telephone

SOUND, words, talk—this was the world of Alexander Graham Bell, an Edinburgh-born, British-educated Bostonian. His grandfather had invented a system for curing stammering; his father had written textbooks on speech; he himself had spent days peering into people's ears to see how they worked. Now in the hot June of 1875 he infuriated professional inventors by inventing the telephone. Since he was not an electrician, they reasoned, he had no business to do it; one of them, Moses Farmer, could not sleep for a week after hearing what Bell had done. A shortsighted Western Union was to turn its back on billions by refusing to buy the machine for $100,000. Only 25 years later, there were more than a million telephones in America, and Bell had ushered in the Age of Unlimited Chatter.

Bell went on to other things—iron lungs, disc phonograph records, hydrofoil speedboats, airplane controls. But nothing in his life ever equaled the crucial moment when, experimenting with his "improved telegraph," an accidental jamming of a transmitting device suddenly showed him how he could send sound over wires.

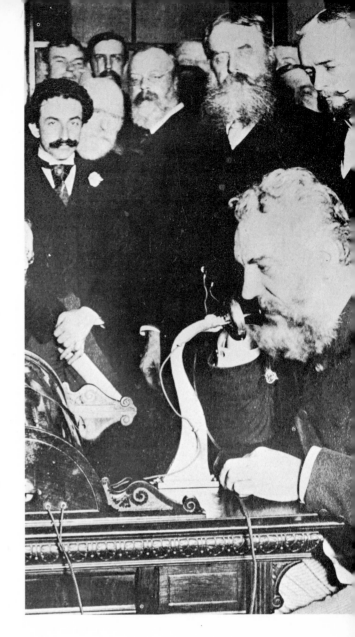

OVER THE LONG LINES Alexander Graham Bell *(right)* makes the first New York-to-Chicago call in October 1892. Clustered around are writers, editors and telephone company executives.

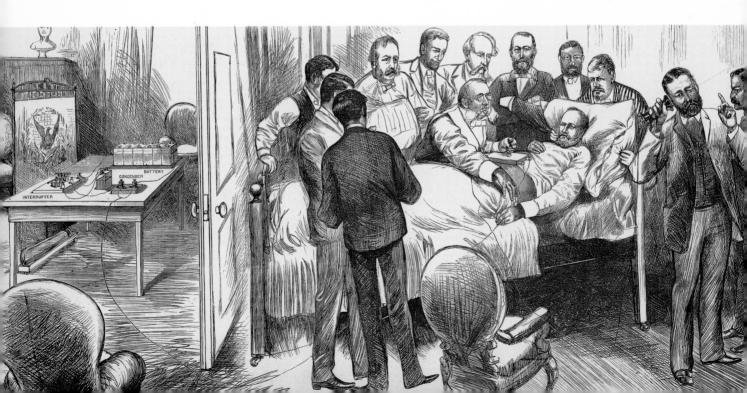

"THE WONDROUS TELEPHONE," an 1877 song, proves prophetic. Of the joking predictions on the cover, only talking to the man in the moon is not here, and now even that seems close.

BULLET DETECTOR (forerunner of the modern land-mine detector) is used by Bell (left) in an effort to locate the assassin's bullet fired at President Garfield in 1881. Elaborate electrical equipment in the adjoining room powers the machine.

A CIRCULAR KITE is flown (right) at Bell's laboratory on Cape Breton Island, Nova Scotia. Flying fascinated him, and his frequent tests with various wing shapes finally led to the aileron, which enables planes to bank and turn with precision.

The dedicated engineers
and their beautiful bridge

CRIPPLED ENGINEER Washington Augustus Roebling uses field glasses to keep track of work from his house. His wife carried his orders to assistants.

Opening night for the new bridge sees great bursts of fireworks and a marine

DARING WORKERS in swinging platforms and bosun's chairs attach suspenders (the steel ropes that support the bridge roadway) to the great cables.

THE greatest engineering marvel of the 19th Century's age of invention was the Brooklyn Bridge, opened by President Chester A. Arthur and Governor Grover Cleveland on May 24, 1883. The bridge, flung 1,595 feet across the East River from Brooklyn to Manhattan, took 13 agonizing years, $15 million and 20 lives to build. It stands in tribute to John Roebling, who designed the span and was killed while surveying its route, and to his son Washington Roebling, who completed it but was crippled for life by working in the compressed air of its caissons. Six days after it opened, its creaking caused a panic and 12 people were killed in a frantic rush to shore. Despite all this, the bridge has won a warm place in the hearts of New Yorkers. Of the great bridges that have since been built around Manhattan Island, many think it remains the loveliest.

parade, climax of a daylong celebration. The tolls were: a penny for a pedestrian, two cents for a sheep, 10 cents for a horse and carriage.

"PRESSING THE BUTTON" on an early Kodak that took circular pictures, Eastman photographs a friend aboard ship in 1890 just as the friend photographs him. These cameras cost $25 and a 100-exposure roll of film was $10 more, including developing. Mass production soon brought a better camera at five dollars and a similar amount of film at just over two dollars.

Kodak cameras are the butt of contemporary jokes such as those (below) in "Scribner's Monthly" in 1889. Like Ford autos later, Kodaks

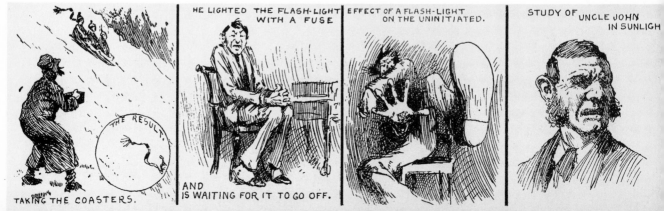

TAKING THE COASTERS.

HE LIGHTED THE FLASH-LIGHT WITH A FUSE
AND IS WAITING FOR IT TO GO OFF.

EFFECT OF A FLASH-LIGHT ON THE UNINITIATED.

STUDY OF UNCLE JOHN IN SUNLIGH

Early Kodak advertising stresses the camera's simplicity. The camera and film were shipped to the factory for processing and reloading.

The man who made it easy to take snapshots

YOUNG George Eastman of Rochester, New York, set out to make his fortune in photography. It took him just about 10 years to achieve his goal. His means were a camera of simple design, roll film provided by skilled chemists, advanced ideas about mass production, and an internationally recognizable word—Kodak—he had dreamed up. Soon everyone was snapping pictures. Kodak factories in America, England, France and Germany were hard put to keep up with the demand for film, and George Eastman was enjoying himself. He gave lavish parties for his friends, vanished into Africa and Europe on hunting and bicycling trips. Everywhere his invention touched and shaped the modern world. Eastman's laboratories created revolutions in medicine, astronomy, journalism, education and the waging of war. He poured at least $100 million in grants into schools and universities. Then came a crippling disease of the spine that threatened all his faculties. Aged 77, he wrote his friends, "My work is done. Why wait?" and shot himself.

AN EARLY EXPERIMENT, this portrait of Eastman, taken in 1884, is annotated with a partial explanation of the photo process. The inventor's handwriting sprawls across the print.

thrived on this humor. A newspaper said cameras added to picnic terrors because people indulging in hilarity would be "caught in the act."

Bright battle on the Bowery

The Bowery, once the center of New York's theatrical district, had fallen on evil days in 1895 when the picture below was painted. However, thanks to a couple of feuding inventors, it glittered. George Westinghouse's generators were driving and lighting the streetcars, and his air brakes brought the elevated

trains to safe stops. His alternating current even lit some of the store windows, although Edison's direct current lit the rest and would soon be driving the elevated trains. Supporters of the Edison system pointed out that it was Westinghouse's alternating current that was being used to kill criminals in the electric chair at Sing Sing Prison, and George stolidly replied: "Alternating current can do no harm unless a man is fool enough to swallow a whole dynamo." Although Westinghouse was forced out of the empire he had created, his alternating current eventually triumphed over Edison's method.

3. CIVILIZING THE WILD WEST

As late as 1847, the American West, between the Missouri River and the Pacific Ocean, was a mighty unknown. After Stephen Long, an army explorer, trekked over the prairies of Kansas, eastern Colorado and northern Oklahoma in 1820, he reported them "almost wholly unfit for cultivation, and of course uninhabitable by a people depending upon agriculture"; on his map he labeled the area "Great American Desert." Farther west and south lay New Mexico and Arizona—empty, forbidding lands.

To the north stretched other grasslands and the tumbled, towering masses of ranges rising to the Rocky Mountains. Through this unmarked and dangerous wilderness—the future states of Wyoming, Montana, Idaho and the Dakotas—a few fur traders and trappers moved with masterly skill as they chased the beaver into their last solitudes. On the Pacific Coast, promised lands beckoned. California, to be taken from Mexico in the name of Manifest Destiny, was known to have pleasant valleys, and from the 1830s on, a trickle of Americans had settled in the rich Columbia River Valley of Oregon. But the Great Plains were largely left to their natural inhabitants. An advancing civilization, which had conquered the forests east of the Mississippi and Missouri, avoided conflict with the Sioux and the Comanche.

Then in 1847, Brigham Young was led "by the Lord's providence," he said, to the vast protected tableland near the Great Salt Lake. Here the Church of Latter-day Saints could be safe from the harassment it had known in Ohio,

TOOLS AND TRAPPINGS used by Texas cowboys trace the workaday history of the cattle industry, whose vast empire overspread the Southwestern plains after the Civil War.

Illinois and Missouri, and within a decade more than 20,000 Mormons were living in the future state of Utah.

Now the pace of the march quickened. In 1848 gold was discovered in California, and swift, almost shattering transformations began. Fortune hunters swarmed like bees to the new El Dorado. In 1858 there were fresh strikes in what became Nevada and at Pikes Peak, near the headwaters of the Platte, where a rough mining town named Denver sprang up. During the Civil War years, new booms brought hopeful gold and silver seekers to mining camps in territories that bore the names of Idaho, Wyoming and Montana. After 1869, when the first transcontinental railroad was completed, the forbidding overland crossing could be made at 22 miles an hour, in plush seats. The "Wild West" faced the beginning of the end.

IN the last quarter of the century, the process of absorbing the West into a national political and economic order took place. It was an energetic and vigorous struggle in which modern technology compressed into barely a generation developments which had required two centuries east of the Mississippi. There was heart-rending conflict in it, for the nation took pride in the beauty of its continental heritage, yet, in the name of progress, hungered for riches attainable only by destroying the simplicity of the wide open spaces.

The swift, intense "civilizing" process created larger-than-life characters—the Indian-fighter, prospector, cowpoke and homesteader—who stayed briefly, and then were gone. As early as 1884, the humorist "Bill Nye" could write that the railroad had put every spot in the West within a day's ride of "where you can get the daily papers and read them under the electric light. That robs the old canyons of their solemn isolation and peoples each gulch with the odors of codfish balls and civilization—it seems sad."

Bit by bit, Indian hunting lands were occupied and resistance snuffed out through superior force; bit by bit, the remnants of the tribes were herded onto reservations—which were guaranteed to the Indians forever, but quickly overrun if they proved to contain anything valuable to the white man. In 1876 the Sioux had created a sensation when one of their war parties surprised Lieutenant Colonel George Custer in Montana and killed his entire command. This massacre on the Little Bighorn blurred the fact that in most of the Indian fighting in the 1860s and 1870s, the army outnumbered the red men, had all the advantages and spent part of its time setting fire to Indian encampments deserted by warriors and populated by helpless squaws, children, the old and the sick. Toward the end, it was simply no contest, for railroads gave the army mobility that the Indians could not match, and savage slaughter of the buffalo by professional hide hunters wiped out the basis of Indian subsistence. Between 1872 and 1874 three million buffalo a year were killed; heaps of stinking carcasses marked the onward path of civilization.

Sitting Bull, the great Sioux leader, was a fugitive in Canada by 1877. (He would later make peace, then be killed by army guns in 1890.) In 1877 Chief Joseph, of the Nez Percé tribe of Idaho and Oregon, surrendered after a bitter winter battle, saying: "I am tired of fighting. Our chiefs are killed. . . . The old men are all dead. . . . He who lead[s] the young men is dead. It is cold and we have no blankets. The little children are freezing to death. . . . Hear me, my chiefs. My heart is sick and sad. I am tired."

By 1885 almost every American Indian had been pushed onto a reservation.

Even though legend places Sitting Bull at the head of the Sioux who wiped out Custer and his men, he was actually a medicine man who stayed behind the lines during the melee; two other war chiefs, Crazy Horse and Gall, won the battle. Later Sitting Bull fled to Canada, where he learned to write. The primitive self-portrait seen below shows him and a bull on a horse.

Geronimo's surrender in 1886 marked the end of serious fighting by the Plains Indians. In 1890 tribesmen on the South Dakota Sioux reservation hearkened to a brave named Wovoka, who had visions of a time when the aged, weary earth would die and be reborn—the white man to another world, the red men to their undisturbed lands of old. The Sioux gathered to prepare for the day with purifications, incantations and proper ritual. The white man called these ceremonies the "Ghost Dances" and his old fears were stirred by the sight of emotion-charged red men. Troops sent in to disarm the Indians first seized hunting weapons, then panicked and used rapid-fire guns to mow down 200 Sioux (many of them women) at Wounded Knee.

Such episodes were the true stuff of Indian conquest. William Cody, "Buffalo Bill," did kill buffalo, but his "victories" over Indians were invented for dime novels and his own Wild West Show. The tales filled a need, for they surrounded an essentially inglorious process with a myth that would save a nation's pride, even when there was no ground for pride.

In 1887 Congress attempted to formalize the destruction of Indian tribal life. It passed the Dawes Act, which authorized the division of reservations into 160-acre family farms; so situated, the theory went, the noble red man would turn into a peaceful farmer, become "civilized" and attain citizenship. Many well-meaning reformers supported the bill as a humane finale to a "Century of Dishonor," during which the tribes had been systematically defrauded of food and payments due them by traders and Indian agents, and hunted down by pioneers and soldiers. Unfortunately, the humane assumptions of 1887 had little relationship to anthropology, history or geography. The Indian was, in most cases, a lost soul when divorced from tribal society. Moreover, much of the semi-arid region where the reservations lay was wholly unfit for small-scale, individual farming; lastly, the Dawes Act proposed to transform the tribe-oriented Indian into a Great Plains individual farmer at the very time when experienced farmers on the eastern rim of the Plains were discovering the incredible difficulties of farming the prairies.

In effect, the act made it possible for large tracts of reservation land not allotted to the Indians to be sold to whites who coveted them. As for allotted land, fast-talking pitchmen swarmed in to bilk Indians of the value of their holdings. One early traveler observed that civilizing the Indian was slow work, and people "who eat their meals in four minutes and a half, and push railway lines across the prairie at the rate of two miles a day, cannot wait a hundred years to give the Indian time to bury his tomahawk, wash his face, and put on a pair of trousers." Nevertheless, the nation entered the 20th Century with confidence that it had "solved" the "Indian problem" and that Plains warfare was frozen into the fading past.

FADING, too, was the individual prospector. When he had rushed to the "diggings" with pick and pan, he could not realize that he would be displaced as surely as had the Indian he drove before him. With modest luck a man could wash $10 to $50 a day out of a stream. With real luck a find might make someone a millionaire. A young Mississippi riverboat pilot named Sam Clemens went with his brother to the Nevada Territory, "smitten with the silver fever" as he was later to recall under the pen name of Mark Twain. And why not? Who could resist, when "Johnny Morgan, a common loafer, had gone to sleep in the gutter and waked up worth $100,000."

Apache leader Geronimo, who terrorized both sides of the Mexico-Arizona border during the 1880s, wound up touring expositions—Buffalo, Omaha, the 1904 World's Fair in St. Louis—selling his photograph (above) for 25 cents. Before his peaceful death, he became a member of the Dutch Reformed Church and took part in Theodore Roosevelt's inauguration in 1905.

The dream of striking it rich only occasionally had some substance. The "Big Bonanza" mine in Nevada's Virginia City yielded up $200 million to four men of Irish immigrant stock—John Mackay, James Fair, James Flood and William O'Brien. And there were other ways to wealth. In one mining camp, profiteering merchants got away with charging $28 a hundredweight for flour and $1.20 a pound for butter—astronomical prices for those days. But for every instance of fabulous success in the boom days, there were countless examples of blasted hopes.

The mining millionaires generally acknowledged the role of luck, and spent with a free hand and a frank ostentation. They wallowed publicly in their money, like H.A.W. Tabor, the Denver mining king who built an opera house, or the Virginia City mine owner who shod his horses with silver. Yet all the gaudiness could not hide the fact that as surface outcroppings of metal were exhausted, mining became a big business involving thousands of feet of shafts, the erection of stamp mills and refineries to process the ore, and great capital investment. A few successful prospectors themselves became the organizers of mining companies. Most often, operations on this scale involved corporate wealth; the more typical pattern of mining by the 1870s was that of Utah, where some 20 companies, capitalized at sums ranging from $100,000 to $2.4 million and owned by absentee capitalists, probed for gold in the Wasatch Range.

T HE change that took place in mining by the end of the century is best shown by what happened in Butte, Montana. In 1881 Marcus Daly persuaded three wealthy men to buy into a once-valuable silver mine, the Anaconda. As it turned out, Anaconda's rich copper, not silver, would determine Butte's future prosperity. By 1889, Daly was making huge profits in copper. He built an entirely new town—Anaconda—to house his smelters, formed the Montana Improvement Company to cut timber on the land grant given to the Northern Pacific, and also poached on government-owned timberlands.

In his struggle to dominate copper mining, Daly came into conflict with William A. Clark, another Montana tycoon. Clark ran for territorial delegate on the Democratic ticket in 1888. Daly, also a Democrat, prodded his miners into voting as he directed, and threw the election to a Republican. Clark bought temporary revenge by spending a million and a quarter in the 1894 election that chose Helena as the state capital over Daly's Anaconda. Then Clark reportedly spent another three quarters of a million to have the legislature choose him United States senator in 1899, only to resign when his election was investigated. In 1901, when echoes of the disputed election had died down, Clark ran again and was re-elected.

By that time Daly had sold out to a new mining corporation, the Amalgamated Copper Company. Amalgamated bought out other mining companies and inherited the war that some of its subsidiaries were fighting against still another copper baron, Frederick A. Heinze. Heinze's specialty was to buy modest surface claims which adjoined producing mines, then cut into the neighboring ore beds through underground tunnels. When challenged in the courts, he diverted some of his ample profits to buying judges for protection, meanwhile loudly proclaiming (not without some truth) that he was battling the "monopolists" who controlled Amalgamated. In 1906 Heinze finally sold

James C. Flood, an astute Irish bartender in San Francisco, listened to his stockbroker customers discussing mines and made fruitful speculations. As his income topped $250,000 a month, he built forbidding mansions like "Flood's Wedding Cake," seen below, in which he lived in increasing seclusion. A fence he built was jeeringly called "the $30,000 brass rail."

out to Amalgamated, which later took the name of Anaconda and finally united all the mines of Butte under one mastery.

Men gambling for hundreds of millions did not let civic niceties stand in the way of winning a lawsuit or an election. They bought judges and legislators. On the labor scene frontier violence lingered and mining strikes were among the bloodiest in the '90s, with unions sometimes using dynamite against strikebreakers. Despite corporate reprisals, organized labor retained its strength among the miners; the pick-and-shovel man working on his own account had become largely a curiosity of the past.

Past and present were mingled in the cattle trade of the Southwest. Although long established, it was given tremendous stimulation just after the Civil War by the new railroads fingering out from Chicago and St. Louis into Missouri and Kansas. The meat-hungry cities of the North could look for beef in the abundant herds of Texas, where steers were plentiful but buyers few. A shrewd Illinois livestock shipper named J. G. McCoy was one of the first to realize that the rails offered a way of connecting what has been called "the four-dollar cow with a forty-dollar market." By the beginning of 1867, McCoy had persuaded the Kansas Pacific Railroad to establish low rates for the beeves to be shipped from his stockyards at a little Kansas station. So Abilene became the first formally created cow town.

Then the word was spread in Texas that steers could be driven to a railhead market over Plains country, with grass and water available and without let or hindrance from farmers or bushwhackers. Herds of inexpensive calves, fed on the plains for a year or two at no cost and sold at Abilene for a thousand per cent increase in value, constituted a fortune on the hoof. In three years, more than a million head were driven into Abilene's pens. The success of Abilene was followed by the development of the northern plains. Reaching from Texas almost to the Canadian border, these unoccupied grasslands, hundreds of miles wide, soon overshadowed Texas in beef raising. Other cow towns flourished, and the cattle kingdom bawled and boomed through the 1870s and into the 1880s.

The cattle drives called into being a new type of Westerner to take his place with the mountain man and the Indian scout. Cattle drovers in the East had walked their beasts to market. Now, with vast herds spread over square miles of grass, the mounted cowboy was indispensable to move the beef from range to railroad. It was a demanding job, for each drive was a sweaty, leathery epic of days and nights in the saddle.

Though the danger from Indians and rustlers was later overrated by romancers, the cowpoke with his spurs a-jingling did carry a gun as the triumphant symbol of his right to make and enforce his own code of behavior. He wore picturesquely functional clothes—broad-brimmed hat against the sun, work gloves for handling reins all day, chaps to protect legs from tangling with brush, high-heeled boots to anchor him in his stirrups. He borrowed the terms of his trade from the Spanish of the borderlands to the south of him, and worked costume, customs and lingo together into the stuff of legend. In retrospect he became not simply an employee who got a dollar a day, plus beans and bacon, for exhausting work. He was enshrined as the mounted man who rode free—tough, alone and unmarred by civilization.

Later generations forgot his debauches in the dance halls and saloons of

THE MAGNETIC ATTRACTION
OF PRECIOUS ORES

Discovery of the great Comstock Lode in 1859 brought 20,000 gold miners to Virginia City, Nevada. In Colorado, reports of silver ore attracted thousands to Leadville and Telluride. Although the gold of Helena, Montana, quickly petered out, the silver and copper ores of Butte provided lasting jobs. In Wyoming the chief gold site was near South Pass City. Santa Rita and Bisbee remain copper towns. Cripple Creek drew gold miners in the 1890s and its mines are still producing. Of the many boom towns in Idaho, Idaho City is one of the few not deserted today.

the cow towns at the end of the trail, or else idealized them. Popular culture, starting with Owen Wister's novel *The Virginian* in 1902, made him the "good guy" who could kill evildoers without legal formalities and yet retain his integrity. He enthralled a nation which wanted to believe that power could be exerted without paying the price in lost innocence. In many ways, the cowboy of fiction and film, less interesting than his counterpart in fact, was the most striking creation of America's last frontier.

For the cattle kingdom *was* a part of a dying frontier. Lurking behind the lean independence of the cowboy was a fateful drive toward organization and mechanization. One man recalled that in 1880 "thousands of buffalo darkened the rolling plains" of Montana and "no one had heard tell of a cowboy," while in 1883 "there was not a buffalo remaining on the range" but "there were 600,-000 head of cattle." Texas alone shipped 4,223,500 cattle between 1866 and 1880. Kansas, Nebraska, Colorado, Wyoming, Montana and Dakota had fewer than 130,000 cattle in 1860, more than 4.5 million by 1880.

In the race to stock the ranges, individual cattlemen were outstripped by corporations, which could pool purchasing power to buy huge "starter" herds. In 1883 alone, 20 stock-raising corporations, whose capitalization totaled $12 million, were formed in Wyoming. English and Scottish investors joined in, forming syndicates that claimed acreages running into hundreds of thousands. With the exception of the invaluable water holes, whose purchase was recorded with every formality, very few ranchers got legal title to such lands. "Title" was defended by illegal fences and, as a last resort, by parties of armed cowhands. Wealthy young Easterners (among them young Theodore Roosevelt) took flyers in Western cattle, and combined business and recreation by going out to supervise their own spreads.

STOCK raisers soon banded themselves into informal organizations to set up ground rules for boundaries, water rights and brands. These groups carried weight; by 1885 the Wyoming Stock Growers Association virtually controlled the region's cattle business. These associations were essentially cliques of those already "in," and charges rang long and loud that their aim was to crowd out newer and smaller operators. But the trade was too far-flung to eliminate competition.

So, in the middle '80s, the bubble burst. As the range became crowded with fresh herds of hungry animals, good feeding areas grew scarce. Cattlemen desperately pumped money into fencing tracts for themselves, recklessly enclosing government lands, Indian reservation lands—any acreages which promised salvation. But in 1885 the Federal government, under Grover Cleveland, relentlessly downed the illegal fences. Meanwhile, prices in a glutted market took a catastrophic tumble. In 1885, cattle that had been expected to bring in $35 or $40 sold at $8 to $10, if at all. Then, in the winter of 1886-1887, the Northern herds were almost completely wiped out by a long, harsh freeze-up that melted away in the spring to reveal heaps of carcasses in every ravine. Northern cattlemen had been warned about those winters, but had shrugged and taken their chances.

With the grand collapse came stabilization. A few open-range holdouts continued to hunt for free grass and now found that fences were being used *against* them by oncoming prairie farmers and sheep raisers, and by cattle ranchers with enclosed ranges. Wire cutters and six-shooters flashed in the

In the early days of the open range in Texas, a yearling calf belonged to any man who could rope and brand it. Soon, to protect the four-footed property, 5,000 brands— initials, numerals and emblems (above)—were registered. Samuel Maverick, who refused to brand his calves, lost a lot of cattle but gave his name to the language, as a synonym for a nonconformist.

moonlight and some blood flowed, but the game was up. Those who succeeded under the new conditions were the prudent souls who saw the handwriting on the wall, secured legal title to their land and read growers' journals for the latest reports on high-quality breeding stock and feed grains.

As the railroad network filled in, the long trail drive became unnecessary. Ranching was, finally, a business. "Cowboys don't have as soft a time as they did," lamented one old hand. "I remember when we sat around the fire the winter through. . . . Now we go on the general roundup, then the calf roundup, then comes haying—something that the old-time cowboy never dreamed of. . . ." And another veteran of the trails, mournfully surveying neatly fenced farms where the cowboy was once the lonely lord of all, was told farmers were "the bone and sinew of the country." "I say, Damn such bone and sinew!" he groaned. "They are the ruin of the country, and have everlastingly, eternally, now and forever, destroyed the best grazing-land in the world." They had, too—and inside of 20 years—with plenty of help from stock raisers who overgrazed the range. Another gaudy facet of Western life was gone.

THERE was nothing colorful about the prairie farmer, who was merely a sunburned symbol of the true riches to be won by honest toil. Long before the Civil War, reformers argued that the true key to democracy lay in providing public land for the yeoman farmer, the backbone of society. If the land were free, then monopoly, speculation, poverty, the arrogance of capital—and all other ills that social flesh was heir to—would disappear. In 1862 this view appeared to triumph in the Homestead Act. Any adult citizen could claim 160 acres of the surveyed public domain, and after five years' continuous residence he could get a final title upon filing a few papers and paying from $26 to $34 in fees. The act was a gallant gesture to the spirit of equality and the honored Jeffersonian ideas of agrarianism, and a symbolic bow to those who worked the soil—God's chosen people. And it had almost nothing to do with the realities of Great Plains agriculture.

To begin with, the Homestead Act itself could not secure fencing material or bring water to the arid plains or break the matted grass roots of the virgin prairie sod. Invention did aid the farmer here. Barbed wire, first produced in 1874, solved the fence problem. Windmills were developed which pumped water from deep-drilled wells. Earlier in the century, John Deere had worked out a new kind of plow. In 1868 this was improved by James Oliver, whose chilled-iron plow was a match for stubborn Plains soils. A host of other farm machines that arrived in the 1870s let horse power and steam power harvest bumper crops with a family-size work force.

The trouble was that the Homestead Act did not provide families with the several thousand dollars needed to buy this machinery. Moreover, the basic 160-acre farm unit was not large enough to raise sufficient crops to give a reasonable return on this heavy capital investment. And its limited area was too small to provide enough water. Finally, neither free land nor new gadgets could save those trusting souls who, late in the '70s, edged out into western Kansas and Nebraska beyond the 98th meridian, where the average annual minimum rainfall would not sustain normal farming. Thousands of these optimistic families limped back in defeat; Kansas editor William Allen White watched a pair of wagons pass through Emporia one day in the '90s, driven by men who had given up "only after a ten years' hard vicious fight . . .

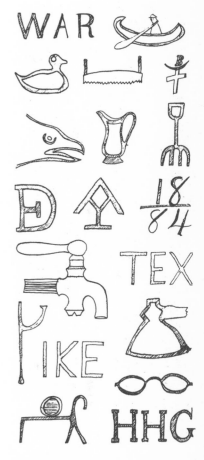

Logs in the Northwest, like cattle in the Southwest, were branded with a wide variety of symbols—including water spigots—like those seen above, for many lumber firms floated their timber on the same river. Downstream, sorters separated logs according to their owners and, as with unbranded cattle (facing page), any maverick log belonged to the sawmill that got it.

which had left its scars on their faces, had bent their bodies, had taken the elasticity from their steps. . . . They had such high hopes when they went out there; they are so desolate now."

Irrigation might have helped, but irrigation usually required joint effort. Co-operative colonies with their pooled capital, like those founded at Anaheim, California, or Greeley, Colorado, might make a go of irrigated farming. So could the Mormons, banded together under tight church discipline in Utah. That was not yet the way of the American farmer.

Even the Homestead Act, the individual farmer's Magna Carta, worked against him, for it was widely used to secure choice land for powerful operators through "dummy" entries. Further, Congress let the act fight for existence among other, conflicting policies. A Desert Land Act of 1877 offered mile-square tracts at $1.25 an acre to anyone who would irrigate them. Cattlemen filed claims in the names of complaisant ranch hands, made token gestures at irrigation and ended with huge parcels. The Timber and Stone Act of 1878 allowed individuals to buy 160-acre blocks of timberland at $2.50 an acre. Timber magnates filed thousands of "dummy entries" which, bought for the price of one good log, produced thousands of feet of marketable boards and shingles.

Congress parceled out over 180 million acres to the railroads along their rights-of-way. The lines, however, could choose which sections they wanted in the reserved strips that ran from 20 to as much as 120 miles in width through which the tracks ran. Controlling this valuable land, the railroads could wait until farmers gave in and bought at railroad prices; to be sure, the land was frequently offered at attractive terms to bring in settlers. Congress also gave the states princely grants under acts to aid education and other public-spirited programs. The Morrill Land Grant Act of 1862 was a forward-looking way of allowing states to endow agricultural colleges with money realized from sales of Federal land grants. Yet the 140 million acres thus donated undercut the Homestead Act's basic principle. The states passed out their shares to speculators, lumbermen, mining magnates—anyone who had the ear of the legislature, as the 160-acre farmer seldom did. In addition, there were state-owned lands that were given away. Texas, always ready to operate on a big scale, handed out three million acres in land-grant and state lands to a Chicago syndicate to create the XIT ranch. In return, the Chicagoans built Texas a state capital costing $1.5 million. The cost of the ranch worked out to 50 cents an acre in a swath that extended for 200 miles.

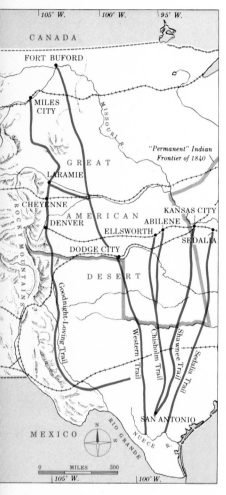

EXIT INDIANS;
ENTER CATTLEMEN

In the first half of the 19th Century the area east of the Rocky Mountains was called "The Great American Desert." Settlers considered it worthless and the federal government therefore turned the land into a "permanent" Indian reservation (north and west of the thick gray line). But when cattlemen found the land would support stock raising, they drove the Indians out. Five railroads soon crossed the territory, and beeves trudged along five cattle trails to cow-town railheads. Then trains carried the animals east to the great packing houses and a hungry nation.

All told, half a billion acres of the public domain had been disposed of by 1900; only 80 million of these acres were patented under the Homestead Act—many of them issued to loggers or cowhands acting as "dummy" entrymen for the boss. No wonder the land giveaway of the 30 years after the Civil War was called a great barbecue, at which those strong enough to elbow their way to the tables got the choicest cuts.

Still the farmers came on. Assailed by drought, they made wry jokes about the man who, when hit with a raindrop, fainted from shock and had to be revived with two buckets of dust. Their hopes remained high. When a large portion of Oklahoma was opened to homesteading in 1889, a thousand eager souls were on hand, on horses and bicycles, in hacks, wagons, carriages and trains, to rush for homesteads at the sound of the starter's gun.

Even while groaning over calamities imposed by God and man—dry soil and bad weather, heavy freight and interest charges, low prices for grain and meat—the farmers accomplished prodigies of food production, flooding the mills and packing houses of Kansas City, Minneapolis and Chicago, and filling the bellies of the world. From 1850 to 1910 American farms grew from 1.5 to 6.4 million. The wheat crop alone climbed from 309,116,000 bushels in 1876 to 522,963,000 bushels in 1896. Other farm commodities kept pace. Even the bounteous production worked against the farmers by lowering prices. But the troubles of the Great Plains farmer did not reflect the state of agriculture everywhere. Between 1860 and 1890, California's fruit, livestock and cereal crops were laying the foundations of wealth that would last when the mines were exhausted. One reason was that the large-scale farm already existed in California. As early as 1873, more than 11 million California acres were in farms of over 10,000 acres, with only 4,663,000 in farms under 500 acres.

The full story of agriculture was complex. If nowhere especially bright, and if not precisely encouraging to the notion that small-scale farming in a large-scale economy could survive indefinitely without help, the tale of the soil was still thought to have a potentially happy ending. At least, the thousands of migrants who kept moving westward thought so. But as 1890 approached, the increasingly angry complaints of the Great Plains farmer could not be ignored. Clearly, he was not a happy and self-sufficient yeoman, and master of his fate, as Jeffersonian thinkers had dreamed of him for 60 years.

AN increasingly settled land, by 1896 the Wild West was cut up into commonwealths—Washington, Montana, the Dakotas, Idaho, Minnesota, Nevada, Wyoming. Even Utah, after a flurry of Mormon resistance over abolishing polygamy, bowed to what its religious leaders considered the unrighteous yoke of gentile government in Washington. Only Oklahoma, New Mexico and Arizona were not yet among the 45 states that ran from ocean to ocean. (Oklahoma would be admitted in 1907; New Mexico and Arizona in 1912.) The new states were not always recognizable as Western versions of the original 13. Vast stretches of unoccupied land remained within their borders. Their populations were small. Sometimes their legislatures bore the stamp of ownership by mining or lumbering interests. But they were in the Union.

It had happened so fast. Conservationists were already worrying whether the forest would soon vanish like the buffalo. Railroad whistles moaned where ox whips once cracked; the cowboy carried hay to barns in winter. The Indians waited, not very expectantly, for citizenship, which was supposed to work some powerful medicine that would feed their hungry children.

A scholarly young man from Portage, Wisconsin, summarized the situation. Frederick Jackson Turner stood before a convention of historians in 1893 and said that the 1890 census found it impossible to trace a continuous line that marked the frontier of settlement. "The frontier has gone," he insisted, "and with its going has closed the first period of American history." A generation or two later, historians would still be arguing what Turner meant and whether he was right about what the frontier had signified in American life. No matter how the argument went, an epoch *had* closed: a gaudy and wasteful epoch of courage, greed, broken daydreams and very genuine achievements. Its consequences were to linger long after the West had undergone the last steps in its "civilizing."

DEERE PLOW

EMPIRE GRAIN DRILL

WILDER PLOW SULKY

EMPIRE THRESHER

The 19th Century saw a revolution in farm implements. John Deere's steel-bladed plow cleansed itself of the caking prairie soil. The grain drill, an early step in mechanization, planted seed in rows and covered it. The plow sulky enabled a farmer to ride as he plowed. The threshing machine, yet another forward step, separated wheat and chaff, and bagged the grain.

The cowboy legend: fact and fiction

During 20-odd years of the late 19th Century, the cowboy rode high, wide and handsome into legend. The starting point was the six million long-horn cattle in Texas. To young Joseph G. McCoy, it was clear that there was money to be made if he could get this cheap beef to a railhead and then ship it to Chicago. By 1867 the pattern was set. And as the cowboy guided his bawling charges along the 1,000-mile Chisholm Trail to McCoy's pens at Abilene (and along other trails to other cow towns), he became the most romanticized American folk hero—the independent man, tall in the saddle, who defied Indians, defended truth and honor with his six-shooter, and wound up his long ride with carefree carousing in tinkling dance halls.

It was not until the 1880s that artists began to immortalize the cowboy. By then, his dominance was being destroyed by his own rape of the open range and by farmers' fences. The best of the pictorial historians—Charles Russell (*The Bolter, opposite*), Erwin Smith (*Herd Formation, below*) and Frederic Remington—had been cowboys themselves. For that reason, their records (seen here and on the pages that follow) faithfully reveal both the glitter and the drabness that have been metamorphosed into the cowpuncher's saga.

A PATIENT COWHAND "trails" his grazing herd north to market at an average of 10 miles a day. The cowboy rode hard to keep the herd compact and needed up to six changes of horse.

A REBELLIOUS BOLTER is deftly roped by a lariat made of 50 to 60 feet of manila or braided rawhide. Cowboys mastered half a dozen throws, each suited to circumstance.

YARNING COWBOYS swap tall stories and drink coffee. Russell, badgered by his wife into giving up his cowboy friends, nostalgically painted himself into this scene *(standing at right).*

TOLL COLLECTORS of the Crow tribe stop an enormous herd crossing their reservation. The cowhands, among whom was Russell, refused to pay, so the Indians stampeded the animals.

Dusty days, starry nights, minor perils, major drunks

To the routine hazards of weather and stampedes, plains folklore added the bloodthirsty figure of the Indian. But the Indian was usually less interested in killing than in stealing a pony or extorting a few steers. Nor were such acts without cause. Cattlemen drove their herds across Indian reservations and grazed them on Indian grass for months at a time. In return, the Indian demanded a toll—sometimes in beef, at others in cash—but trail bosses often refused to pay and provoked the Indians' last small acts of hostility. Charles Russell's painting *(below)* shows the dusty prelude to one such event. In other works, idyllic and inebriate, the artist rounded out the picture of a trail-rider's life.

THIRSTY RIDERS enter a saloon without dismounting. Here they found release from months in the saddle or bunkhouse life, so boring that time was passed shooting flies overhead.

CHOKING ON DUST, the "drag riders" bring up the rear of the herd, eyes open for ailing and laggard cattle. This was the least desirable position and was generally assigned to beginners.

CHARGED WITH FURY, a bronco rears. Months were required to turn a wild horse into a trained cow pony. The training was thrill-packed. Riders bet heavily on their ability to sit the horse.

A unique record
of the wrangler's hard life

Parched by summer heat, lashed by winter's howling northers, the cowboy labored hard for his dollar a day and keep. From spring roundup and branding of newborn calves to fall sorting of beeves for the drive to market, his days were long and arduous. On the trail, two of the top riders, the "pointers," led the herd and prevented mixups with other outfits heading for the railroad. The other riders were strung along either side of the line of animals that sometimes stretched for miles, or brought up the rear. For fun the men competed to see who was best at broncobusting or at roping and throwing steers—a part of their everyday work that developed into the modern rodeo.

Some of the best photographs of cowboys at work and at play were taken by a self-taught Texan, Erwin Smith. Smith's enormous knowledge of his native state and his years of cowpunching experience were a rare combination. But to this he added an innate artistry and produced the revealing shots, some of which appear here, that commemorate the nomadic life he loved.

CAUGHT AT BOTH ENDS, a calf is branded to establish ownership and foil rustlers. But absentee owners lost many calves to unscrupulous cowboys who burned on their own brands.

65

The cowboy's best friend

The small sinewy mustang favored by the cowboys seemed born for herding and, once broken to the saddle, needed no coaching to nip at a balky cow's flank. The cow pony's instant responsiveness is illustrated in this Smith photo of a cowboy as he separates, or "cuts," a steer from the herd for branding

or sorting. The cowboy would select a cow (he called all cattle cows, regardless of sex) and use his pony to jostle it into the open. Sometimes the cow would swerve abruptly and then the cutting horse would pirouette quickly, a movement called "turning on a dime," and also the title of this picture.

The most valuable mounts in the horse herd were those that worked well at night. And so prized were good horses that in the alkali lake regions many cowboys carried canned tomatoes to make the mineral-filled water palatable to their horses, although they themselves would drink the acrid water straight.

Cowboys ride hell-for-leather into town to spend their pay. Buildings like this general store are now the hallmark of Western movies.

SHOOTING CRAPS on a bedroll passes an off-hour on the range. The dice thrower at right is easily identifiable as a green newcomer by his clean white shirt with sleeves neatly rolled up.

QUENCHING THEIR THIRST are hands from Smith's outfit, the LS Ranch. Aside from gaudy kerchiefs and snakeskin hatbands, there is little resemblance to the tall cowboy of myth.

The pursuit of pleasure in the open range country

THERE are less cutthroats and murderers graduated from the cowboy," said a Dodge City mayor, "than from the better class who come from the east for venture of gain." But when the cowboy came off the trail, he fired his six-gun with a somewhat unnerving abandon. Smith's photos show other leisure-hour scenes.

The cowboy's gamut of town pleasures was rather limited. He could indulge in made-to-order boots at $25 (ready-mades were only $10), he could drink, he could pass time with the dance-hall girls. At the ranch or on the range he sang, gambled, whittled or fought. To stop violence, one ranch banned the possession of "any pistol, dirk, dagger, slingshot, knuckles, Bowie knife or...similar instruments for...offense or defense."

RELAXING in a dugout adorned with horseshoe, coyote hide, elk horn and dirty towel, cowboys prepare for a hunt. The game they shot gave some variety to the chuck-wagon menu.

QUIRTS FLYING, quarts under their belts, six-guns popping, four cow-punchers are forever fixed in bronze in Remington's well-known sculpture entitled *Coming through the Rye*.

Texas longhorns: explosives on the hoof

The fabled longhorns, a legacy of the Spanish explorers, were running wild when early settlers in Texas discovered them. Wild-eyed and panicky, longhorns stampeded at the least unexpected noise, trampling one another. The worst stampedes occurred by dark, so cowboys on the night watch dreaded electrical storms. When the herd erupted, the cowboy raced ahead, as seen in Frederic Remington's *Stampede by Lightning* (owned by the Gilcrease Institute of Tulsa), and tried to turn the cattle into a circle until they tired. Afterward, the cowhand had reason to let off steam *(above)*.

4. ORGANIZED LABOR TAKES FORM

IN July of 1876, citizens of Philadelphia proudly gazed at the nightly torchlight parades in honor of Independence Day, another aspect of the celebrations capped by the Centennial Exposition. Just one year later, the skies of Pittsburgh, 300 miles to the west, were lit with a different glow. A mob of thousands, supporting Pennsylvania Railroad workers out on strike, raged through the streets and set fire to the Union Depot, shops, offices and hundreds of freight cars. There was a chilling significance in this tale of two years and two cities. The first fruits of America's second century of independence seemed to be class warfare and social revolution.

However, the American laborer was far from ready to take to the barricades, although he might be driven, in desperation, to fling a cobblestone at a strikebreaker or a policeman. In 1877, he was still in the throes of adjustment, for the age of mass production, which uprooted so much, was perhaps hardest on the man who made things with his hands. It turned him from a skilled craftsman into a unit in a production process that began with the unloading of raw material and ended with a crate of finished goods. The steps in this new process were numerous and small and often done by machine. There were many more "specialties" in labor—but fewer crafts. As a craftsman, the American workingman had walked with dignity in his community. Now his role was diminished and the pride he had in his skill was losing its meaning.

What was more, the new modes of production were striking at another

A MACHINE POLITICIAN is the role President Chester A. Arthur is chiefly remembered for. But he signed a progressive bill creating the Bureau of Labor demanded by unions.

cherished American belief: that working for wages itself was acceptable only as a steppingstone to ownership. In 1859, Abraham Lincoln had clearly stated this credo to a Wisconsin audience. "The prudent, penniless beginner in the world labors for wages awhile, saves a surplus with which to buy tools or land for himself, then labors on his own account another while, and at length hires another new beginner to help him. . . . If any continue through life in the condition of the hired laborer, it is not the fault of the system, but because of either a dependent nature which prefers it, or improvidence, folly, or singular misfortune."

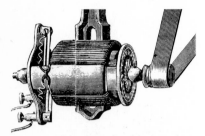

T WENTY years after that speech, it was evident that even the most prudent beginner in the world stood little chance of buying the millions of dollars' worth of tools which made up a factory. The current was running swiftly the other way. The hired worker was not only shorn of his expectations of becoming a capitalist, but as shops increased in size he was lucky if he knew by sight the capitalist who employed him. "Well, I remember," said one disgruntled brassworker to an investigator in 1883, "that fourteen years ago the workmen and foremen and the boss were all as one happy family . . . but now the boss is superior, and the men all go to the foremen."

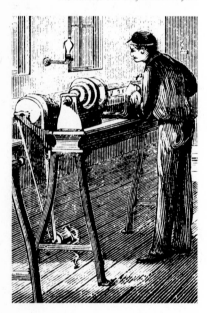

A primitive electric motor (above) operates equipment in a machine shop (below) in this 1882 illustration. Although the first electric motor was built by Michael Faraday in 1831, he had no interest in it as a practical tool. Half a century later the alternating-current motor, which revolutionized industry, made its public debut powering the humble but useful electric fan.

A jarring change in hopes and status had to be faced and dealt with, somehow, in terms that would make sense to Americans. Labor's problem was not purely an abstract one of social recognition. Though wages rose during the Civil War and postwar boom, they often lagged behind rising prices and did not always quickly catch up. Then, in 1873, a sickening depression hit the nation. Employers slashed pay while holding men at work an average of 60 hours or more per week. The striking railroad men of 1877 were protesting against pay cuts that would slice their average earnings by 10 per cent, this on top of previous wage cuts and widespread unemployment.

New England textile workers in 1883—when the country was some years past the worst of the depression—earned from 50 cents to $1.80 a day, and such skilled workers as shipwrights only managed to get between $2.60 and $3.50 a day. In 1884, the state of Illinois found that the average yearly earnings of the head of a family were $525.27. With annual living expenses estimated at $507.56, little surplus was left for enjoying the fullness of life, though a man could substantially increase family income if he put his wife and children to work.

Wages were not the whole story, either. Unsanitary and unsafe conditions were the norm in a factory system built with frantic haste, for quick profit, by a nation-on-the-make that believed in hard work and no frills. Sometimes a workman got his pay, after a long wait, in orders on a company store that sold plain goods at fancy prices, or had to pay stiff rent on a company shack in a mill or mining town. Worst of all was a feeling of helplessness among workers, because a man who argued or quit was getting to be easily replaceable. "A man who had served an apprenticeship of five years might be brought in competition with a machine run by a boy," one labor leader noted in disgust, "and the boy would do the most and the best." Or a workman could walk in one morning and find his bench taken by someone else—perhaps one of the foreigners who were showing up in greater numbers every year.

In fact, under the Contract Labor Law of 1864 the employer could recruit such foreigners in gangs from overseas. In California the American workman might have to compete for his job against low-paid Chinese coolie immigrants —in other states, against convicts who were either leased to private employers or whose goods, turned out in prison shops, undersold the goods of free laborers and destroyed their jobs. Coolie, contract and convict labor were powerful discouragements to complaint. And in the end, perhaps this loss of control of the situation was what hurt the most.

For despite pay scales that fluctuated with the pulse of business, even depression wages bought things, thanks to mass production, that had been luxuries not long before—ready-made clothes, gaslight and newspapers, cheap cigars. The real income of each gainfully employed member of the population actually rose 8 per cent in the '70s and 11 per cent in the '80s. But to be dependent—to be made a pauper tomorrow on the whim of a boss or by a vagary of the mysterious market—this was what was intolerable in free America.

Even before the Civil War it was becoming clear that the answer for labor was to organize and consolidate, as business itself was doing. Clear though the solution seemed, it raised many complex questions that were to be debated for the rest of the century. Organize how? And to what end? Should American laborers collect around the cores furnished by the few craft unions of the time? Or should they obliterate divisions among different skills and join with all workers of a given industry or region to press their demands? Once organized, what weapons should they choose? The strike? The boycott? If these worked, should their demands stop with higher wages? Or should labor push for the abolition of the wage system entirely and fight to replace it with co-operative ownership of industries, or even with one of the newer kinds of socialism which were under excited discussion in Europe, so that all would have a better break in the economic struggle? Should there be an attempt to join with farmers and other productive workers in political actions? (It may sound farfetched to modern ears, but such a course might then have won support from farmers and even small businessmen.) And if so, should political activity be through the older parties or by new ones, and with what platforms?

From 1860 to 1895 answers to all these hard questions were sought as the labor movement took shape through trials and tempests. What finally emerged as "organized labor" was, understandably, a rather tough organism. But it was somewhat stunted, and twisted into a shape that made it hard for theorists to classify or idealists to love.

ALMOST from the beginning of the nation's industrial development, there had been a clustering of skilled workmen in local unions. In different cities typographers, cordwainers, stonecutters, machinists, cabinetmakers—specialists all—pledged themselves in mutual brotherhood to resist wage cuts or the introduction of too many apprentices. They paid monthly dues into strike or sick-benefit funds and sometimes controlled conditions in their trades. The Civil War saw a brisk increase in such local organizations in the North, and by 1865 there were over 270 such brotherhoods.

As early as 1827 a few labor organizers had looked ahead to a next step, the leaguing of the various skilled locals in one city in a trades assembly that would serve as a general headquarters and an educational and propaganda center for workingmen of every specialty. This was an attractive notion, and during the 1830s the trades assemblies flourished.

There was another possible form of large-scale combination of workingmen.

IMPORTED, DUTY FREE, by TRUST, MONOPOLY & CO. TO COMPETE WITH AMERICAN LABOR.

Newly arrived immigrants, hired as strikebreakers, are the target of this cartoon reflecting the attitude of angry American unionized workers. One coal-mine operator armed a group of Italian newcomers in 1875 and told them to shoot any striker who came near. Two men were killed and the guilty immigrants jailed for murder. The mine-owner was fined five dollars.

The various city locals of a single craft might be united into a national trade union. In 1850 the typographers formed the first national. During the years that followed, as the railroads turned the shops of an industry into a nation-wide producing and selling system, the logic of national unions became evident. By 1864 there were national unions of blacksmiths, iron molders, hat finishers, stonecutters, cigarmakers, carpenters. Some 32 such "nationals" had enrolled between 170,000 and 300,000 workers by 1873. The nationals were neither tightly organized nor rich, but they had grand visions and a soaring style of nomenclature. The iron puddlers named themselves the Sons of Vulcan; the shoemakers, equally allusive, became the Knights of St. Crispin. And as soon as unions gained a few locals in Canada, they added the glorious adjective "international" to their name.

THE growth of the nationals did not seriously threaten the trades assemblies, which by 1865 existed in almost every important industrial center. As the Civil War ended, there were major differences between trades assemblies and the national unions. The assemblies were interested in fusing men of different skills in a single movement and in using political action to achieve their goals; the national unions were concerned more with craft unionism and economic gains. The conflict would be resolved by the next obvious step—federation on a nationwide basis which would determine the look and possibly the objectives of organized labor.

At the outset, however, and in fact until the '80s, it did not seem to make much difference who was in the van. The leaders of all the earliest gatherings of labor spokesmen were primarily social reformers and political agitators; they, like most workers, could not conceive of the existence of a permanent wage-earning class which needed a special consciousness of its role in history and politics. Whether they spoke as delegates for trades assemblies or nationals, they were alike in calling for a unity of all producers, including laborers, farmers and small businessmen; in embracing cure-all policies which would purge society of every possible evil which restrained it from flowering into utopia; alike in their faith that workers might somehow manage, in large-scale industry, to be self-employed; and, lastly, alike in their heavy reliance on political education and action as labor's best weapons, rather than the strike.

The scouts and advance parties of the labor movement from 1865 to 1880 included men like William H. Sylvis of the Molders' International Union. Born in a Pennsylvania village, he had been a journeyman foundry worker, then a part owner of a business, then a worker once again when hard times struck. As president of his union, in 1868, he told its annual convention that hard times were no accident. "The cause of all these evils is the WAGES SYSTEM. . . . We must adopt a system which will divide the *profits* of labor among those who produce them." The proper system, Sylvis thought, was one of co-operatively owned foundries, which would "restore confidence, renew hopes, and give a reasonable promise of . . . freedom from strikes and taxation." Another spokesman for the workingman of the '70s was Martin Foran, organizer of the Coopers' International Union. In addition to learning the barrelmaker's trade as a young man, he had picked up some higher education and an urge to better himself. Within four years after organizing the coopers he became a lawyer in Ohio; shortly thereafter, he served as city attorney of Cleveland and after that as a congressman for several terms.

A lucky Chinese loses only his pigtail in an 1880 Denver race riot. The fighting probably began when a Chinese laundryman slashed a customer over a 10-cent underpayment. In the melee, one man was hanged and the city's 400 Orientals were hunted mercilessly until militia restored an uneasy peace.

Then there was Charles Litchman, the onetime Grand Scribe of the Knights of St. Crispin. He was born in the Massachusetts fishing village of Marblehead in 1849. His father was a small-scale manufacturer of shoes, and Litchman learned the trade from him. It was a useful acquisition, for after a fling at studying law and an attempt at going into business for himself, he found himself at work in a shoe factory. Undiscouraged, he joined the shoemakers' union, ran twice for the Massachusetts legislature as a Republican and was twice beaten. In 1878 he switched to the Greenback ticket and won a term. By the '90s, however, he was a practicing Republican again. Even those who thought that *any* labor union spokesman was automatically tainted with the poisonous foreign theory of class consciousness would have had a hard time attacking the pedigree of Litchman. This joiner in a nation of joiners was in his time a Mason, a Grand Senior Sagamore of the Great Council of the United States Improved Order of Red Men, and a member of the American Legion of Honor and Order of the Golden Cross.

Any national organization founded by men like Sylvis, Foran or Litchman was bound to be freewheeling, ambitiously political, and anything but restricted to the woes and wants of wage earners. In 1866, at Baltimore, 77 delegates from trades assemblies, from local and national unions, and from clubs organized to lobby for an eight-hour day, formed the National Labor Union. The meeting adopted a report which opposed strikes, "except as dernier resort," and took a strong stand in favor of its most important goal, the eight-hour day. But it also spoke up for a national labor party (the time and manner of organization left unspecified), co-operative stores and workshops, and the reservation of the public domain for actual settlers. A committee solemnly called on President Andrew Johnson to present these decisions and was received with courtesy but no promises.

The next year, the National Labor Union convention added a new plank to its platform. Declaring that the "money monopoly is the parent of all monopolies—the very root and essence of slavery," the delegates endorsed an inflationary monetary policy. Although this doctrine of "greenbackism" had been initiated by small manufacturers and farmers, enough labor voters endorsed greenbackism to give it a million votes in the 1878 congressional elections. Labor leaders hoped that the movement's promise of easier credit would enable craftsmen to hold on to their independent trades and reduce the number of wage earners competing for jobs. In advocating more free land for settlers, the N.L.U. was voicing the belief that potential wage earners, given the opportunity, would turn from the factory to the farm. Both ideas were hopelessly out of touch with the facts of industrial development.

NONETHELESS, the leaders stood firm in their faith that such catch-all programs would line up support for labor among all those groups with a grievance against the changing order of things. In 1868 they accepted delegates from women's suffrage organizations; in 1869, Negro delegates; in 1872 they finally launched their party, the National Labor Reform party. But the structure of the party was too ambitious for its time. The national trade unions were unable to reconcile their economic aims with the increasingly political tendencies of the N.L.U. In 1871, the craft unions sent no representatives to the N.L.U. convention. Lacking effective leadership after the sudden death of Sylvis, the N.L.U. and its party soon collapsed.

Charles Litchman was a leader of the Knights of St. Crispin, the shoemakers' union, the first skilled craft group to be endangered by the use of labor-saving machinery. The Knights were also threatened by convict labor, which led to Litchman's campaign for a label to identify union-made goods.

Uriah Stephens, head of the Noble and Holy Order of the Knights of Labor, was so fanatical about secrecy that in public announcements five stars were substituted for the name of his organization. Stephens opposed predatory employers because "living by and on the labors of others is dishonest."

The N.L.U. was followed by other groups, all protesting the ills that laboring flesh was heir to. Seventy representatives from sundry unions met in 1873 and constituted themselves an Industrial Congress, but after two more meetings (in the grim depression years of 1874 and 1875) the congress failed to emerge with any clear-cut program of action. The Industrial Brotherhood (birth date unknown, death in the '70s) and the Sovereigns of Industry (born 1874, expired 1880) formally approved more organization and co-operation— but could do little to implement their words. In 1878, however, the Workingmen's party of California, determined to exclude Chinese laborers, captured some seats in the state legislature.

Meanwhile, in 1869, a Philadelphia garment cutter named Uriah Stephens had met with a handful of fellow clothing workers in an effort to revive their declining union. Out of their discussions came the Noble and Holy Order of the Knights of Labor. The order was secret, to protect its members against the serious threat of employer reprisals. Stephens, who knew some Greek through his training for the Baptist ministry, and who was also a Mason, an Odd Fellow and a Knight of Pythias, devised an elaborate ritual. There were officials with names like Inside Esquire, Master Workman and Venerable Sage; secret grips and passwords; and a seal full of symbols for justice, wisdom, truth, industry, economy, the races of man and the divisions of the earth. A candidate was brought in the dead of night to an unknown address, testified to his belief in "God, the Creator and Universal Father," took a solemn vow of loyalty, standing in a circle with other members, and was welcomed "on behalf of the toiling millions of earth . . . to this Sanctuary."

Today this may all seem like childish falderal. But the Knights were in deadly earnest and their mumbo-jumbo titles helped conceal the identities of members who, if known, would have been blacklisted. There was, nevertheless, something moving about these early labor organizations. To be a Sovereign of Industry or a Knight of Labor made a worker stand a little taller. For the Knights, industry was more than foremen and factories; it was the productive toil of brothers—a way of life. Today a Knight of Labor might work in a hot, dark sweatshop and eat his lunch on a packing crate amid cloth scraps, metal filings, leather snippets, spittle, shouts, the squeak and rumble of unprotected machinery. But tomorrow, tomorrow he and his brothers—yes, the capitalist, too—would stand clean and proud before machinery that they owned, recognized as creators of value, heroes of production in a wholesome society with no poor and rich, no oppressors and victims.

IT was slightly mad, but no more mad than the dream of farmers who, just at this time, were joining a new society called the National Grange of the Patrons of Husbandry (better known as the Grange) and listening while orators envisioned the yeoman, in clean overalls and with no manure under his nails, humbling the moneylenders by co-operative purchases of reapers. It was, in fact, no loonier than a good many dreams which had already come true in America, a land that sometimes seemed to exist purely to deny the probabilities of history. This time, however, the impossible could not be achieved. There was no room in the modern world for an industrial machine owned piecemeal by co-operative associations of independent craftsmen. What technology had joined together, reform could not put asunder.

The weakness of the labor movement of the '70s was cruelly revealed by the

Capital and Labor, "just showing how strong they are," hack away at the bridge of Prosperity, bent on destroying each other. In the theoretically classless society of the 1870s, it appeared to many that there was a growing "chasm between capital and labor." Roscoe Conkling, however, blithely poohpoohed the rift, saying that there was no chasm, only "sar-casm."

five years of depression that began in 1873. Most of the trades assemblies and national unions then existing went under. The nationals declined from some 30 in the early 1870s to eight or nine in 1877; locals, beset by layoffs and lockouts, shriveled and died. The cigarmakers, the textile workers and the coal miners all suffered heavy setbacks through unsuccessful strikes. An investigator for the Philadelphia and Reading Railroad (one of the larger mineowners) uncovered a secret organization known as the "Molly Maguires" which, it was asserted, beat up or murdered mineowners and straw bosses, and at times gave the same treatment to workers who were unwilling to obey strike calls. The "Mollies" were much overplayed, but the trial of a number of their alleged leaders, in 1875 and 1876, prepared some people to believe that sinister and violent men dominated unions. Those fears fed amply on the explosive railroad upheavals of 1877.

THE trouble began with a series of pay slashes that compounded other grievances of working railway men. Times were hard—bread lines and soup kitchens were part of the urban scene—and the railroads were becoming the symbols of corporate villainy, though only yesterday they had been lauded as the spearheads of progress. At any rate, on Monday, July 16, 1877, strikers on the Baltimore & Ohio spontaneously walked off their jobs; there had been no strike call by their union. The next day, a walkout created a blockade of stalled trains at Martinsburg, West Virginia, and men at other points on the line soon quit work. On Friday, Governor John Carroll of Maryland decided to send the state's National Guardsmen to protect railroad property at Cumberland. When the soldiers marched to the Baltimore depot, a mob filled the streets, threw cobblestones, fired shots, swarmed over the tracks and kept the troops from leaving. In the answering fire, 10 workers were killed. Federal troops had to be hustled in and by Sunday night, there were some 500 armed soldiers on duty in Baltimore.

Meanwhile, with memories of the Philadelphia Centennial still green, Pennsylvania Railroad workers in Pittsburgh struck, though without any conscious co-ordination with the B & O trainmen. On Saturday, July 21, a Philadelphia militia unit arrived to take things in hand, for the Pittsburgh militia had proved unwilling to fight the mobs. Twenty thousand raging men—railroad workers, unemployed artisans and a probable leaven of riffraff—besieged the hated Philadelphia kid-glove Sunday soldiers who had taken shelter in a roundhouse. Nearly 50 rioters and some of the soldiers were shot before the militiamen finally made their way, under fire, to safety. Mob rule lasted for four days, while the strike hit Altoona, Harrisburg, Reading, Johnstown and other places. The Erie and the New York Central were struck too, and militiamen, aided by local police, struggled to keep order.

In Chicago a mob of thousands fought police in the streets and presently the city was patrolled by almost two regiments of regulars, two state-militia companies, small detachments of artillery and cavalry, and about 5,000 special deputies. In St. Louis, a so-called Workingmen's party closed the town down for about five days in what came close to a general strike. The outbreaks even reached to the West Coast, and in San Francisco the unrest took the characteristic form of a riot against the Chinese.

To most newspapers and other public spokesmen, this was revolution, and the New York *Times* epitomized the general level of vituperation when it

In this 1874 cartoon, Thomas Nast joined Labor and Capital as indivisibly as Siamese twins. While Nast saw that unity was essential, others did not. Editor Edwin Godkin felt that every man was "competent to make his own bargains"; the famed preacher Henry Ward Beecher called unions "the worst form of despotism and tyranny in the history of Christendom."

described the rioters variously as blacklegs, looters, communists, rabble, law-breakers, tramps and bummers. *The Nation*, then the mouthpiece of political respectability, urged that the allegation of labor's right to interfere with strike-breakers should be "refuted with gunpowder and ball," and it was. President Hayes met daily with his Cabinet for more than a week at the end of July and announced that United States property would be protected at all costs. Taking advantage of this ambiguous statement, railroad companies attached mail cars to freight trains in the expectation of federal support.

IN Pennsylvania the governor, assisted by 3,000 federal troops, personally saw to opening up the line between Philadelphia and Pittsburgh, and rode into the steel city in command of four troop trains, with the lead locomotive pushing a flatcar on which a Gatling rapid-fire gun was mounted. By July 30 more than 10,000 state and federal troops were on duty between Pittsburgh and Blairsville—and everywhere strikebreakers were being protected and strike leaders arrested. As August opened, the strike was in ruins. Under those ruins lay the idealistic hopes of the '60s and '70s for a grand union of all the productive classes which would purify society without conflict. A new labor organization would have to be forged, and two organizations emerged as contenders for labor leadership.

The first of these was Uriah Stephens' Knights of Labor. During the bleak '70s the Knights were building a structure based on local assemblies. These were composed either of workers in a single trade, or else were "mixed," with a variety of crafts contributing members. Locals were gathered into district assemblies—and again, these could be mixed, or else composed exclusively of local assemblies of workers in a single trade. In 1878 the district assemblies called a national meeting, at which a constitution was drawn up. The delegates also authorized a resistance fund to finance strikes, co-operatives and education, to be built up out of contributions by the locals, and called for arbitration of labor disputes. Further, they asked for purely political reforms, such as the establishment of state and federal bureaus of labor statistics in order to get accurate information on industrial wages and prices to use in bargaining.

The first national gathering of Knights also wrestled with the question of whether or not to abandon secrecy, and finally voted to remain mysterious. But it was evident that changes were coming and in 1879, Grand Master Workman Uriah Stephens resigned and suggested Terence V. Powderly as his successor. Powderly remained the leader of the Knights for 14 years.

He was a man bred for controversy. Born of Irish parents in Carbondale, Pennsylvania, in 1849, Powderly was trained as a machinist. Despite this humble background, he was fixed in the tradition of middle-class self-improvement that underlay the attitudes of reformers and conservatives alike in mid-19th Century America. While he was advancing in the Knights, he studied law (even though the organization at first barred lawyers, bankers, doctors, professional gamblers and liquor dealers from membership) and he continued to advocate producers' co-operatives, the end of land monopolies, inflation and other general cure-alls. Before becoming Grand Master of the Knights he had been elected mayor of Scranton, Pennsylvania, on the Greenback ticket. He spoke and wrote for temperance reform and land redistribution. One journalist, noting Powderly's glasses, mustache, double-breasted broadcloth coats

A Granger meeting held outdoors resounds with flowery oratory. When the embattled farmers turned their guns on political and economic targets in the 1870s, the response was drastic. Jay Gould, owner of a number of railroads, was so incensed by complaints about high freight rates that he toured the Midwest in a special train, threatening to end service.

and high collars, declared that "no one ever drew such a looking man as the leader of a million of the horny-fisted sons of toil."

In one sense, Powderly belonged with the utopian visionaries of the 1840s, rather than with the wage workers of modern industry. On the other hand, he was a practical leader who gradually pruned the Knights of their cabalistic trappings and began to turn them into a truly national labor organization—open, irreproachable and widely based in its membership. By 1881, Powderly was able to end most of the order's secrecy, thus dispelling the suspicions of many middle-class Americans that all secret organizations were terroristic, like the Molly Maguires.

The relaxation of secrecy also permitted Powderly to dispel the hostility of the Roman Catholic Church, which had been suspicious of this secret organization with its religious ritual. Anti-Catholic crusades like the Know-Nothing party had, in the past, begun in precisely this fashion. But Powderly was careful to keep Catholic leaders informed of the true purposes of the Knights, and in 1886 even convinced Cardinal Gibbons of Baltimore to intercede for the organization at Rome when it looked as if the Holy See might forbid Catholics to become Knights.

UNFORTUNATELY, the American labor force was not uniformly receptive to the middle-class idealism symbolized by Powderly and the Knights; labor was riven by disputes between the immigrant (who often spoke a strange tongue) and native, the skilled and unskilled, the Negro and white, the Southerner and Northerner. Craft unionists shied away from the Knights' interest in women's rights and co-operatives; the locals' main concern was for better hours, legislative protection, and higher wages—through the strike when necessary, and Powderly was reluctant to strike.

This reluctance, or perhaps lack of understanding, went to the heart of the mystery as to Powderly's aims. Once the workers were organized and politically educated, what did he want them to do? The question was thrust upon him in embarrassing form in 1885. As the result of a threatened strike by local assemblies of the Knights made up of railroad men on the Union Pacific and the Southwestern System, the union secured an agreement from the struck railroads to negotiate certain issues and to reinstate any members of the Knights who had been fired during the walkout.

Since the owner of these roads was Jay Gould, the very symbol of aggressive capitalism, laboring men got the idea that the Knights of Labor had slain Goliath. Immediately a stampede to join the Order was on. Membership shot from approximately 100,000 in 1885 to more than 700,000 in a year. At one point, applications for charters for local assemblies were coming into the central headquarters in Philadelphia so rapidly that all organizing work was suspended for more than a month. There were locals composed of women; there was at least an entire district assembly of Negroes (in Richmond) and there were even locals in England, Belgium, Australia, New Zealand and Ireland. The grand march of united workers was about to begin, but Powderly marked time in 1886. Then, suddenly, another leader appeared.

That other leader was Samuel Gompers, a man as sinewy and argumentative as Powderly, but with a shrewder knowledge of the economic realities of the '80s. Gompers was the son of Dutch Jewish parents who emigrated to England, where he was born in 1850. Brought to the United States as a boy

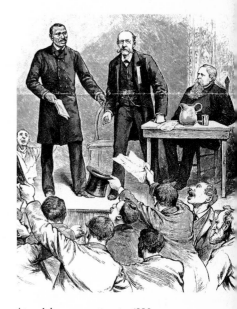

At a labor convention in 1886, Frank Farrell, Negro member of the Knights of Labor, introduces Grand Master Workman Terence Powderly. A mixture of idealism and snobbishness, Powderly could talk of "emancipation from wage slavery" and "sufferings of the masses," then complain that at a picnic he had had to mix with a crowd of noisy, dirty union men.

of 13, he worked with his father at cigarmaking. In small shops scattered through New York's East Side, young Gompers sat at his bench and listened receptively to the chatter of a colorful group of veterans of labor and socialist struggles abroad as they discussed lines of battle that existed in the '70s. The followers of Karl Marx wanted the trade unions to educate workers to move toward abolishing private ownership of the means of production; the disciples of Ferdinand Lassalle, on the other hand, advocated a primarily political approach to creating a noncapitalist society.

Gompers listened carefully to the arguments, bided his time, thought his thoughts and was finally influenced most strongly, perhaps, by Adolph Strasser, who became president of the Cigarmakers' International Union in 1877. Gompers himself was, from its earliest days, a proud member of Cigarmakers' International Union Local 144—and, it should be added, carried a Knights of Labor card as well. Strasser, a Hungarian by birth, had been a charter member of the Lassallean Social Democratic Party of North America, founded in 1874. As time went on, however, and the Cigarmakers' membership rose, the argument between the spokesmen for "trade union socialism" and "political socialism" was drained of its meaning for Strasser. What was wrong, he reasoned, with a trade unionism like the Cigarmakers', which was aimed at nothing more than improving the working conditions of members in the here and now, leaving the future to shape itself?

BY 1883 this conviction had hardened into a philosophy, and Strasser told a Senate committee on labor that the cigarmakers were "opposed to theorists." He declared: "We have no ultimate ends. We are going on from day to day. We are fighting only for immediate objects—objects that can be realized in a few years. . . . Yes, we want to dress better and to live better, and become better citizens generally." Such a program was in tune with the generally pragmatic temper of American life.

Gompers absorbed this simple trade union philosophy from friends and associates like Strasser; like Ferdinand Laurrell, a Swedish immigrant and onetime revolutionary; or like the eloquent organizer of the Brotherhood of Carpenters and Joiners, Peter J. McGuire. As Gompers rose in the ranks of the Cigarmakers' International, he revealed a number of assets—a trenchant pen, common sense and incredible energy.

While Gompers' star was rising early in the '80s, the national trade unions were reorganizing after the debacle of the preceding decade and evolving new policies. Priority went to the creation of larger strike funds; this would give the unions the economic means with which to back up their strongest weapons, the strike and the boycott. The ends for which these weapons were to be used were strictly limited to those promising immediate benefits: the eight-hour day, abolition of child and convict labor, controls on immigration, and the ending of wage payment through requisitions on company stores.

At Pittsburgh in 1881 a group of nationals took an obvious next step by establishing the Federation of Organized Trades and Labor Unions, with Gompers prominent on the organizing committees. The federation, which was primarily a lobbying organization, did not pull as many unions into its fold as it had hoped—not even with its declaration, in 1884, of disagreement with "those theorists who would ignore present social conditions and who strive to direct the labor movement in pursuit of some will-o'-the-wisp mil-

In city slums a new labor force evolved: the tenement workers. Mothers, children and cripples worked in their dismal rooms, making barely enough to live. Employers profited hugely; they had no overhead and paid incredibly low wages. But slums bred disease which was easily spread—in one instance by a consumptive licking glue on cigarettes he was making.

lennium." That was a shot at the socialists of every variety, and also at the Knights of Labor, which was still talking about co-operatives.

The Knights sent representatives to the federation's first meeting, then pulled back warily. From 1882 to 1886 the control of the labor movement hung in the balance, while the leaders of the federation (the printers, cigar-makers and carpenters) and the heads of the Knights bid against each other to line up the unorganized. Theoretically, nothing prevented "dual union-ism." Workers, like Gompers himself, were members both of craft unions and assemblies of Knights. Actually, there was a limit to how much money and leadership could be spared for organization, and every local assembly (partic-ularly of a single craft) organized by the Knights destroyed a potential local of a national craft union. More significantly, if two nationwide organizations existed, there would be a conflict of authority in times of strikes. Therefore the nationals insisted that they must have final and exclusive jurisdiction over their crafts. Soon the leaders of the nationals were angrily accusing the Knights of "stealing" workers and enrolling them behind its broad program which was, in essence, anti-trade union. The fight was on.

The fundamental differences between the Knights and the nationals were deep. The Knights were still thinking in terms of ultimately aligning all the "producers" behind sweeping social reforms. The breaking point, to the na-tionals, was Powderly's belief in an all-inclusive grouping of craft unions with the other elements of an industrial society and the fact that he never quite understood the effectiveness of the strike as a weapon.

The unions following Gompers, Strasser and McGuire were readier to set-tle for the half loaf—to use the weapon of the strike among skilled workers for benefits in the here and now—and let the unskilled, and the rest of society, reap the incidental benefits later. A second difference was in leadership. Terence Powderly had an elaborate, theoretical program, but was short on execution. Samuel Gompers was short on theory, but long on pragmatic abil-ity to win limited objectives. And in labor as well as in the organization of industry, the day belonged to the hard-driving man with a plan who acted first, then rationalized.

At the start of 1886 it appeared as if the Knights were going to be the win-ners, hands down, for they were undergoing a great expansion. That same year the Gompers group attracted only 25 delegates to its Columbus, Ohio, convention. Then events suddenly exploded.

THE federation's 1884 convention had passed a resolution declaring that from May 1, 1886, on, eight hours should constitute a legal day's work. But the convention left it to member unions to decide what they would do to make the resolve a reality. The Knights were invited to co-operate. By 1885 it was clear that a number of unions intended to strike for eight hours the next May. Powderly, however, urged his local assemblies to shun the walkout (advice which a number of them ignored) and by April 1886 he appeared to have missed his chance to capitalize on a popular idea. To add to his troubles, a fresh strike on the Southwestern railway system broke out. This time Jay Gould was determined to outlast the workers, and he did. After the beaten strikers went back to work on May 4, membership in the Knights melted away on Gould's railway lines. Then came the Haymarket bomb.

The full story of this tragic affair will never be known. Among certain

Samuel Gompers, leader of the American Federation of Labor, was no radical or revolutionary. "Our labor movement," he said, "has no system to crush . . . noth-ing to overturn." Gompers stub-bornly plugged for the small raise, the shorter work day—practical gains which would eventually lift ". . . man and woman from the sloughs of poverty and despair. . . ."

workmen in Chicago, primarily Germans, there was a small corps of radical anarchists. They were enemies of capitalism who despaired of trade-union action, possibly even despaired of socialism as the instrument to end the oppression of man by man. And they believed that justice would not triumph until the wicked machinery of the state was disassembled, piece by piece. That process must begin with violence: force to answer the force of armies and police; terror and dynamite to respond to guns. The men who talked and wrote in this manner were a demented handful; they had not achieved even a sizable explosion by 1886. But they were loud and they were frightening.

During February of 1886, workers at the McCormick Harvester plant in Chicago had struck in protest against the firing of union members. In turn, they had been locked out. On May 3, a crowd of these locked-out workers attacked strikebreakers as they were leaving the plant. Police joined the fracas and killed several strikers. August Spies, a member of the anarchist International Working People's Association, was present. He rushed to have a circular printed that called for revenge. A protest meeting was held the next night in Haymarket Square. Speeches were launched into the torchlit air, but nothing more violent than oratory seemed to be in prospect.

The crowd was drifting away when a police detail suddenly appeared to break up the meeting. Just as quickly a bomb was lobbed—no one has ever found out how or by whom. There was a shattering explosion, followed by a crackling of shots from the police. Seven policemen died; at least 60 people, including many bystanders, were wounded. A wave of hysteria swept Chicago and the country. In a passionate atmosphere, eight anarchists were arrested and tried for the crime on a loose indictment containing 69 counts, including murder, conspiracy and riot—though nothing was ever proved connecting any of them with the throwing of the so-called "anarchist made" bomb. One received a 15-year term; seven were condemned to death. Of these, one committed suicide, four were hanged and two sentences were commuted. The three survivors were pardoned in 1893 by Governor John P. Altgeld. One of those executed, Albert Parsons, had been a member of the Knights of Labor (and of the Socialist Labor party and of many other revolutionary groups, including the Confederate Army).

Though Powderly desperately repudiated Parsons—at least publicly—not all members of the Order accepted this disclaimer. Nor did Powderly's action save the Knights from the general wave of reaction and of distrust of all labor-reform organizations which followed the affair. No one can assess just how much Haymarket had to do with the sudden decline of the Knights, but the fact is that from 1886 onward, it went into a slump as remarkable as its sudden climb. The membership tumbled from 729,677 on July 1, 1886, to 259,518 on the same date in 1888.

WHILE the Knights were fading in national importance, the revived trade unions were making a fresh start at federation. The convention held at Columbus in December of 1886 absorbed the dying federation into a new organization, to be known as the American Federation of Labor. The AFL was to include existing unions willing to join, plus trades assemblies, trades councils, central labor unions, state federations or any kind of labor organization which put trade-union objectives first. However, the national unions, which preserved their autonomy, dominated the new group. The

In upstate New York pretty women picket a struck factory. For the most part women were badly treated and underpaid, and unscrupulous employers sometimes refused, for trumped-up reasons, to pay at all. The defrauded women might try to collect; usually they accepted their loss as just another burden.

organizational structure was, consequently, loose. But there were to be a paid president and a fund at the disposition of the Executive Council to support strikes and lobbies as necessary. The first holder of the office was Samuel Gompers, and he remained its president (except for one year) until his death in 1924, on the way home from a convention, allegedly with the words "God bless our American institutions" on his lips.

From the start, the AFL acted as if it had come to stay. It sent emissaries to the Knights, offering to recognize the older organization provided that the Order got completely out of the business of organizing any craft in which the AFL had an interest. The Knights declined to become a cadaver voluntarily, but they did not last long. In 1892 the AFL had risen to a membership of a quarter million. In 1893, when the Knights numbered fewer than 75,000, Powderly was ousted by a combination of socialists and agrarians within the Knights (he became an immigration official under McKinley and Theodore Roosevelt, and died the same year as Gompers). Although practically extinct, the Knights lingered for several decades.

By 1904 the AFL had over 1.6 million members, and Gompers was as well recognized and accepted a national figure as, say, Booker T. Washington— and, like that Negro leader, was the accepted spokesman for a sizable minority. The go-as-you-please, national-craft-union-controlled, limited-objectives approach of the AFL suited the temper of the times. The federation never had entirely smooth sailing, and Gompers was even briefly ousted in 1895. But his conciliatory and organizational skills fitted the vital needs of American labor in this period—to organize, to secure firm contracts and to strike to achieve desired ends.

An angry sweatshop owner browbeats a girl, perhaps for working too slowly. In dingy firetraps, women slaved as much as 84 hours a week to make the few dollars coveted by swarms of unemployed. It was this overabundance of underpaid women that helped slow the improvement in labor standards.

THE development of labor unions in the late 19th Century was a triumph with limitations, and one made possible because of the limitations. Although the AFL's constitution began with a preamble that seemed as fiery as any socialist manifesto ("Whereas, a struggle is going on in all the nations of the civilized world, between the oppressors and the oppressed of all countries, a struggle between the capitalist and the laborer . . ."), the Gompers-Strasser program of "going on from day to day" was clearly the one which would cull maximum support from the already-organized, and meet the least resistance from government and public opinion. The program of the AFL did not promise the millennium, nor in some years did it even deliver much on its limited commitments. Rail and steel and coal strikes would be broken, and injunctions and antitrust actions would hobble unions while the AFL protested impotently.

But it was a nucleus, and a living one. It had come to terms with the reality of permanent industrialization, the deep American attachment to capitalism, and the lack of class consciousness among the scattered and polyglot American laboring force. The Knights of Labor had made significant contributions to organized labor in the creation of a group of men proud to be card-carrying members. But the year 1886 marked an end to the era of labor organizations led by men full of middle-class faith in universal social betterment. It was another farewell to the high visions of the earlier 19th Century, a stage in the growing up of both America and the laboring classes. Like all growing up, it had its pain, its loss, its acceptance of what had to be and its wistful wondering about what might have been.

A maltreated working girl tells her complaint to an interested official of the Working Women's Protective Union. By 1870 the union's small staff of volunteer lawyers was handling hundreds of cases a year and had successfully sued recalcitrant employers for thousands of dollars of unpaid wages.

FRANK LESLIE'S ILLUSTRATED NEWSPAPER

No. 1,390.—Vol. LIV.   NEW YORK—FOR THE WEEK ENDING JUNE 17, 1882.   [Price 10 Cents.

MARYLAND.—THE LABOR STRIKE IN THE CUMBERLAND REGION—MERCHANTS IN THE MINING TOWN OF FROSTBURG CLOSING THEIR STORES BY ORDER OF THE KNIGHTS OF LABOR.—See Page 257.

TOLLING A CURFEW, an errand boy *(left)* for the Knights of Labor rings his bell in the streets of Frostburg, Maryland, in 1882. A shopkeeper is closing in compliance with union demand. Such displays of strength were unusual in labor's early years.

CALLING A MEETING to consider a strike, two miners *(opposite)* use a rock to map the rendezvous for other workers to see on leaving the coal pits. The 1880s, when there were more miners than jobs, witnessed many long and bitter strikes.

The violent years of labor's youth

W HEN a man is steady and sober, and . . . finds himself in debt for a common living, something must be wrong." Thus did one worker express the confusion and the hardship that beset workers everywhere in the 1870s and 1880s. In seeking "an honest day's wages for an honest day's work," they were torn between many methods and many leaders. Radical Johann Most offered one cure for all employers—"Extirpate the miserable brood!" But Eugene Debs, one of the moderate majority, denounced class warfare and held that "those who engage in force and violence are our real enemies."

In practice, labor found that the strike was "the only weapon it possesses of maintaining its rights," and that strikes led to violence. There was grim truth in a chilling remark by tycoon Jay Gould: "I can hire one half of the working class to kill the other half." Hundreds died in fierce clashes between striking workers and strikebreaking workers. Incalculable property damage was caused by general rioting as strikers fought guards hired from the Pinkerton Detective Agency, police, state militia and federal troops. Imperiled and outraged, the public indiscriminately blamed organized labor for the acts of looters and extremists. Antilabor bias ran strong in most newspapers and even crept into their artists' news pictures, examples of which appear on these pages. Though the trade-union movement slowly won recognition, popular opposition insured the loss of many desperate battles along the way.

Hard times for miners, and a vain year-long strike

THE depression that followed the Panic of 1873 was a desperate time for the coal miners. In primitive mines they labored from dawn to dark in constant danger of disaster (below), crippling injuries and lung diseases. Their wages barely supported a family when they worked, and work was sometimes limited to 130-odd days a year. They were so easy to replace that a strike by them was an empty threat.

In Pennsylvania the Miners' Benevolent Association did obtain minimum guarantees from the mine operators' Anthracite Board of Trade. But in December 1874, the operators cut wages below the minimum, and the miners angrily left the pits for "the long strike." The operators imported workers from Europe and strong-arm crews to protect them. These strikebreaking tactics set off a small war and roused the Molly Maguires to their campaign of terror. But in the end, labor was the loser. By 1876 the miners had been starved into submission.

TRADING SHOTS with striking coal miners on a hillside, a Pinkerton guard holds his ground while three foreign strikebreaking workers scramble to a safe spot inside an Ohio mine shaft.

Rescuers reach the victims of a mine fire at Avondale, Pennsylvania, in 1869. A whole shift perished, leaving 59 widows and 109 orphans.

BATTLING EVICTION, the wives of striking miners vainly attack a sheriff's posse in front of their company-owned homes in Pennsylvania. Besides owning many houses, mine operators and industrialists often controlled local schools, stores, utilities and law enforcement. Such "company towns," though benign in concept, usually reduced the workers to helpless subservience.

A "labor revolution" that rode the railways

I N 1877 new wage cuts added a last straw to railhands' grievances. Trouble started in July in West Virginia, where strikers *(opposite, top)* halted 70 trains and formed a huge blockade. Then rioting engulfed Baltimore *(opposite, below)*, Pittsburgh, St. Louis, Chicago and San Francisco. "It is wrong to call this a strike," said one newspaper, "it is labor revolution."

In fact, it was neither a revolution nor a single strike but a chain of independent local eruptions. Only in Pittsburgh did a labor captain *(below)* attempt to coordinate strikes elsewhere. To end the violence in Pittsburgh, 650 troops seized the depots, but by dark a huge mob routed them with a gigantic fire *(right)*. The trouble ended as suddenly as it began. By August most of the strikers were back at work. For the first time since Jackson's day, federal troops had been used to quell strikes.

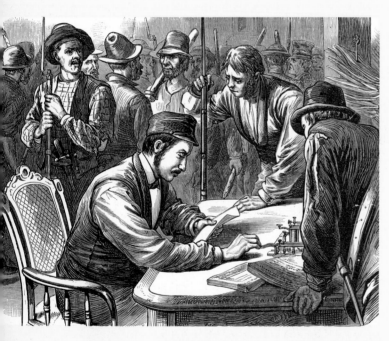

RESOURCEFUL LEADER Robert M. Ammon directs strikers in Pittsburgh and telegraphs orders to others in Fort Wayne. He tried in vain to protect railroad property from incendiaries.

MUSHROOMING FLAMES billow up from a roundhouse in the Pittsburgh freight yards. A wall of fire three miles long destroyed installations valued at six million dollars.

STRIKING TRAINMEN haul the crew from a freight train at Martinsburg, West Virginia. When local militia fraternized with the strikers and refused to fire on them, federal troops had to be called in to break up the strike.

RIOT-BOUND SOLDIERS of the Sixth Maryland Regiment, battling through Baltimore toward the railroad station, fire point-blank at strikers and unemployed sympathizers. City-wide rioting lasted four days, took 50 lives.

A streetcar strike and the Pullman boycott

DISCONTENT on the railroads, unallayed by the many strikes of 1877, boiled over again and again in the next two decades. In 1886 New York streetcar workers *(below)* won their strike for higher wages. Then in 1894 a powerful strike radiated outward from the Pullman sleeping-car works near Chicago. Supporting the strike, the new American Railway Union, led by its founder Eugene Debs, ordered its members to deny clearance to

Wielding clubs to break a strike, 250 policemen open the way for a New York trolley. At this show of force, 15,000 more trainmen struck;

trains carrying Pullman cars. Bitterly fought in Chicago (*pictures at right*), the boycott almost succeeded in spite of federal troops brought in to guard the mails. But Debs was enjoined not to prolong the strike, then charged with contempt for disobeying the court order. With its leaders in jail, the strike wavered and, after two months, collapsed. The addition of the injunction rounded out the basic arsenal of antistrike artillery.

later, all got their pay increased to two dollars for a 12-hour day.

A FLEET OF BOXCARS, set ablaze during the Pullman strike, burns fiercely in a Chicago yard. With rail traffic snarled, supplies dwindled and a meat famine threatened the Midwest.

A ROW OF TENTS, home for troops in the Pullman strike, lines a Chicago street. Famed artist Frederic Remington, sketching the strike for *Harper's*, damned it as a "rape of government."

WITH STOIC RESOLUTION August Spies sits in his Chicago
cell awaiting his execution. He and the six other condemned
anarchists proclaimed their innocence and defiance to the end.

But two of them had the sentence reduced and one committed
suicide. Thus on November 11, 1887, only Parsons, Engel and
Fischer joined Spies before the hangman (*opposite, below*).

As the Haymarket bomb explodes in their ranks, Chicago policemen sent to break up the anarchist rally start firing wildly into the crowd.

The Haymarket bombing and a vindictive trial

ON THE GALLOWS, four Haymarket anarchists aspire to martyrdom in their last words. Said Fischer, "This is the happiest moment of my life." Cried Engel, "Hurrah for anarchy!"

I N 1886 some maverick unions went on strike for an eight-hour day. They were joined by anarchists who hoped thereby to spread their gospel of violence. Soon Chicago was torn by clashes between strikers, strikebreakers and police. It was to protest the shooting of four strikers by police that the anarchists called a rally in Haymarket Square on May 4. When police arrived, an unknown hand heaved a bomb. Its blast *(above)* and the rioting that followed killed 12 and wounded many more.

Eight leading anarchists went to trial for murder. The state's attorney demanded, "Convict these men, make examples of them, hang them, and you save our institutions." The judge distorted the law in his charge to the jury. Swayed by the prevailing hysteria, the jury condemned seven to death. Organized labor disavowed the anarchists but failed to shed the "millstone of odium."

ON HOMESTEAD'S BATTLEFIELD, a soldier peers through the shield from which strikers had fired a cannon at advancing Pinkerton men. The chain (*foreground*) anchored the cannon.

Lockout and lost strike at Homestead Steel

IN July 1892, a new labor battle was joined at Carnegie Steel's Homestead works outside Pittsburgh. The Amalgamated Association of Iron and Steel Workers refused to accept a wage cut. Carnegie's tough general manager, Henry Clay Frick, saw a glowing opportunity to smash the union. He locked up the plant and hired 300 Pinkerton guards. When the guards arrived by boat, armed workers were waiting for them. In 13 hours of skirmishing, 10 were killed and dozens wounded. Finally the Pinkertons surrendered and were run out of town. But the strikers were unable to cope with the subsequent influx of troops and process servers. After 20 weeks they gave up and tried to get back their jobs.

A sensational sidelight to the strike was provided by Alexander Berkman, an anarchist unconnected with it. Furious at Frick's use of strikebreakers, he decided to kill the man. His attempt (*right*) succeeded only in inflaming antilabor sentiment. But even as the Homestead defeat dealt steel unions a 40-year setback, the American Federation of Labor was beginning to grow, showing workingmen the way out of labor's darkest days.

In his Pittsburgh office, Henry Frick (left) is shot by Alexander

Berkman. The Russian-born anarchist spent 13 years in prison and was later deported—the very day that Frick died of natural causes.

5. A NEW DAY
FOR THE
OLD SOUTH

THE audience seated at the long banquet tables set up in Delmonico's Restaurant in New York City on December 22, 1886, was a select one. General William T. Sherman was there, and T. de Witt Talmage, the popular preacher; J. Pierpont Morgan, Russell Sage and a cluster of other millionaires. The New England Society could count on attracting the best men of society to a dinner celebrating the Pilgrims' landing on Plymouth Rock. Full-fed, the guests sat back amid the curls of cigar smoke to listen to the toasts and speeches. Talmage spoke, then Sherman; and then the president of the society introduced Henry Woodfin Grady, a round-faced, smooth-shaven man still in his thirties, as someone who had come "all the way from Georgia."

Grady, editor of the Atlanta *Constitution*, son of a Confederate soldier who had died in action, rose to his feet. He looked at General Sherman, who had burned large parts of Atlanta only 22 years before. He looked at the audience of "fat and jocund sons of New England" who had prospered while he, Grady, and his fellow Southerners struggled through the poverty of Reconstruction. Then he began: "There was a South of slavery and secession—that South is dead. There is a South of union and freedom—that South, thank God, is living, breathing, growing every hour."

Twenty minutes later he sat down amid a storm of applause, having given one of the most popular speeches of the century. His opening quotation had been from former Confederate General B. H. Hill; his next-to-closing one was

NEGRO CONTRIBUTIONS to America are symbolized by three freed slaves: crusader Sojourner Truth *(top)*, educator Booker T. Washington, scientist George W. Carver.

Henry W. Grady, progressive editor of the Atlanta "Constitution," was a leader of the "new South." Among the prewar customs he derided was the reverence for family lineage because, he explained, "I once studied my family tree and gave it up when I found several ancestors hanging from the limbs."

from Daniel Webster, repeating a hope that Americans North and South would remain "united . . . citizens of the same country, members of the same government; united, all united now and united forever." He had struck a note of reconciliation that his audience had been waiting for, and he had painted a portrait of a "new South" whose soul was "stirred with the breath of a new life." It was natural that editorials in newspapers both North and South should hail his achievement with almost synchronized cheers.

For history, however, his omissions were as significant as what he said. He had glossed over one of the underlying premises of his talk; namely that the new South urgently requested and would handsomely repay investment by Northern capitalists. He had not mentioned—if in fact he fully understood—that the new South was still, in spite of a brave façade, a land of poverty and anguish, of pride and fantasy, of hopes and dilemmas and contradictions.

The ending of Reconstruction had restored the right of the South to be, once more, fully American. Yet to be American after 1877 meant to be in love with the future, the machine, the whirl of change; to be buoyant, optimistic and unbeaten. The South *had* been beaten. It reached toward the future but felt that to abandon its past was a betrayal of its dead. It clung to its un-machined ways, and its lands and slow-moving rivers still exercised a spell that yielded reluctantly to "progress."

Southern men and women did not adapt well to the uprooting ways of the age of railroads and factories. Above all, white Southerners feared changes of any kind that could lead to the most dreaded and most resisted change of all—anything which would threaten, in their biracial world, the fabric of white control of Southern life—a control which might be cruel or benevolent depending on time or place, but which in their view had to be unquestioned. (The few whites who did not share this view neither succeeded in, nor long remained a part of, Southern life.)

As a new Southern leadership looked about for ways to restore the section to something approaching a vigorous economy, the balance sheet showed some impressive liabilities. For the most part, investment capital was scarce. Cotton crops were larger, but cotton was not the road to greatness it had once promised to be. The Southern farm worker was poor and likely to remain so as long as sharecropping retained its stultifying primacy.

The South did have untapped assets—great tracts of land that might yield other products than cotton, many thousand square miles of fast-growing timber, rich mineral deposits, willing hands. Gradually a movement took shape to bring the rewards of industrialization to the South. In Alabama the exploitation of Southern Appalachian iron deposits was producing a "Pittsburgh of the South" at Birmingham. The processing of tobacco was becoming a major industry. Lumber and turpentine companies began to work amid the pines of Georgia, North Carolina and Mississippi. A movement to bring textile mills closer to the cotton succeeded in making the mill town a landmark of the South by 1895, as it had long been of New England. All of this growth was triumphantly displayed as evidence of Southern regeneration and reintegration into national life.

For Southerners *were* Americans, and hungry as any for the juicy fruits of an expanding economy. Therefore, in the post-1877 South, life moved to disjointed rhythms. In the cotton fields hoes swung in timeless arcs, while not far away sawmills whined. Men caught catfish in streams which, farther down, turned factory spindles. Men's minds, too, showed a curious tension between old and new, fear and hope. Grady himself could, in October 1888, paint for a Dallas audience a vision of a South "thrilling with new life . . . the home of fifty millions of people; her cities vast hives of industry"; yet eight months later at Charlottesville he could see sinister portents facing the republic in its second century. "The fixed stars are fading from the sky," he said, "and we grope in uncertain light. . . . Established ways are lost, new roads perplex. . . . The cities are swollen and the fields are stripped. Splendor streams from the castle, and squalor crouches in the home."

Could Grady hope that the South would somehow escape these contradictions once its cities, too, became "hives of industry"? Or was there a touch of fear showing through the booster's mask? Whatever the answer, the Southern leadership of the '80s had to reconcile some powerful opposing pulls. Among its techniques for this task were one-party government, and the exploitation of the twin legends of the Old South and the Lost Cause.

THE war dethroned King Cotton only temporarily. He got back on his throne with a series of bouncing crops. By 1877 production had reached its prewar peak of nearly five million bales; by 1880 the cotton crop was 6,357,000 bales, and by 1894, about 10 million—though in that year the price dropped to a disastrous four and a half cents a pound. Tobacco, another long-time Southern staple, more than doubled its production in the 25 years after the war—from 316,495,000 pounds in 1866 to 647,535,000 in 1890. Sugar cane, rice, corn and hay all played their part in the Southern agricultural story too. But cotton brought in the bulk of the Southern farmer's income and, paradoxically, cotton was becoming more of a burden and a curse to that same farmer with each passing year of the waning century.

Cotton surpluses trapped growers in the wreckage of a collapsing price structure which, by the 1890s, was already threatening to fall below the bare cost of production. Moreover, continued cotton culture left men and soil alike thin, bleached and worn out. Southern agriculture needed to experiment with new crops—cereal grasses, citrus and other fruits, peanuts, poultry, vegetables—which could all grow in the humid and hospitable climate. Near the century's end, especially on the outer edges of the old Confederacy—in Virginia, Florida, Texas—such crops were tried, and with success. But in large parts of South Carolina, Georgia, Tennessee, Mississippi, Alabama, Louisiana and Arkansas, the old ways held firm.

To experiment with new crops landowners needed risk capital or state aid. Neither was readily forthcoming in the years after 1877. State moneys went elsewhere, to promoters and industrial developers. In a cash-starved Southland, farmers could secure much-needed annual financing by one or both of two methods. Under the crop-lien arrangement, future crops were pledged as security against advances. In sharecropping, a tenant farmer agreed to share with the landowner the proceeds of the crop.

However, the holders of crop liens, many of them country storekeepers and traders, would only bet on a sure thing. They insisted that the mortgaged harvest should be cotton, for which there was always some kind of market. Since the merchant-moneylender generally made his loan not in cash but in the form of periodic advances of supplies (meat, meal, seed, fertilizers, stock,

North and South, linked by industry, march before President Garfield and his defeated Democratic opponent, General Hancock. But the prosperity Nast drew in this 1881 cartoon did not touch all of America. In the South new industries flourished—and sent profits to their absentee Northern owners.

harness and tools), he could increase his markup on these items enough to protect himself when cotton prices skidded. When he did so, he claimed that he himself was only the victim of the large-scale suppliers of "trust-made" goods, and of the shippers and bankers who gouged *him*. Whether or not he spoke the truth, he had a flexibility in his pricing that was denied the farmer.

During Reconstruction a good many large plantations had been divided up among Negro and white tenant sharecroppers, creating a false impression of spreading economic democracy. Where there had been one plantation, there might now be five farms—but the five new farmers were tenants. The sharecropper who lived from year to year on expectations, tilling other men's soil with other men's tools, was on the way to being a peasant. By 1910 tenants operated more than half of the farms in eight Southern states.

Then, too, there were merchants who found it convenient to foreclose on their landowner-debtors, take over the farms and hire sharecroppers directly. So to the existing evils of the sharecropping and crop-lien systems, the drawbacks of absentee ownership were added. Those who worked the land did not possess it; those who held it in law did not live on it. The result was neglect and the absence of even "such scant efficiency, planning, responsible supervision and soil conservation" as the prewar plantation had provided. The vaunted revival of Southern agriculture produced "exhausted soils, small crops, poor roads, decaying bridges, unpainted homes and unkept yards," one observer noted. He could have added malnutrition and apathy. Small wonder that in 1906 the average annual productive power of an Iowa farm worker equaled $1,088.11, that of a South Carolina farmer $159.75. It was not a cheerful harvest from 11 years of Reconstruction and 30 years of Redemption.

THE problems raised by poor whites and bad farming practices were not new, for prior to the war, voices had proclaimed salvation in the coming of the factory system. Posterity has not yet produced a monument to South Carolina's William Gregg, an industrialist and prophet, but 15 years before the Civil War he was fulminating against the horrors of one-crop agriculture: "unpainted mansions,—dilapidated cabins with mud chimneys and no windows,—broken-down rail fences,—fields overgrown with weeds." Gregg's proposed solution was to build textile factories using Carolina water power to process Carolina cotton and bringing Carolina hill farmers to live next to the mills and work in them. In no time, Gregg promised, the "emaciated, pale-faced children" would bloom in health, family tables would be supplied in rich variety, and a Sabbath visitor, watching "the females turn out in their gay colored gowns," would imagine himself "surrounded by groups of city belles." Gregg built a factory surrounded by a mill town at Graniteville, South Carolina, in 1846 and made it pay, though the records do not reveal much about the success of his hopes for turning poor whites into cheery villagers.

The South was unready to listen to the voices of its Greggs in prewar days. Now, in the 1880s, it was undergoing a change of heart (too late to bring any satisfaction to Gregg, who had died in 1867). A movement to lure cotton mills southward swept the towns of the Carolina and Georgia Piedmont, that region of gentle hills and swift streams. Preachers, lawyers, editors and store-keepers ransacked their bank accounts, bought stock in local factories and begged others to join them. The local textile industry, one newspaper insisted, was "a fine exemplification of what Southern brains and energy, devoted to

Tobacco, the principal money crop of the upper South in postwar years, was processed mostly by hand. The hanging leaves are "air curing." At benches workers pick cured leaves from the stalks and then remove the woody midrib. Negroes in tobacco factories sang as they worked, becoming so proficient that factory choruses were standard attractions at state fairs.

business and consecrated to God," could accomplish. A community patriot is described as having built a mill so that his town might have about it a populace of "happy, God-fearing, working people, enjoying all the conveniences and comforts of improved social conditions." The profit motive, in fact, was rarely mentioned, as if it were slightly indelicate. "We make American citizens, and run cotton mills to pay the expenses" was the way one promoter put it.

Under such benign promptings textile manufacture did increase in the South. Between 1880 and 1890 alone, the number of spindles increased from half a million to more than a million and a half. Nevertheless the road to paradise was not opened, and the basic problems remained basic. By the 1890s, however, mills tended more and more to be operated, and in some cases built, by Northern capital. Northern concerns were reaping the profits of Southern industrialization. Dividends went to Boston and New York banks.

The worker soon found that mill-town paternalism wore thin. Living in a rickety cabin and getting his pay (from 40 to 50 cents a day in North Carolina) in slips exchangeable for meal, meat and overalls at the company store was not much of an improvement over scratching out a living in the hills.

The poor white who came to the factory bench (and only whites were invited by cotton manufacturers) had merely traded one squalid environment for another. He brought with him his fundamentalist preachers and his rural prejudices against change; he jolted himself dizzy with white mule on Saturday night and endured repentance and hell-fire sermons on Sunday. He was the "docile, intelligent, God-fearing American laborer" that Southern spokesmen depicted to woo Northern capital. He was also the original for the caricatures found in Erskine Caldwell's *Tobacco Road* and *God's Little Acre*.

The sordid working conditions of the cotton mill town were equaled by those in lumber camps and sawmills. There the free laborer often had to face the competition of a convict lease system common to the poverty-stricken states of the postwar South. Under it, penitentiary inmates were farmed out to construction, lumbering, mining and other companies which needed plenty of heavy, unskilled labor. The employer paid the state a fee and took over the care and feeding of the working convicts, who could neither strike nor resign nor complain. The result was incredible mistreatment and brutality; the convict camps compared in horror with the worst prisons of the Civil War—perhaps even the slave ships—and had an annual mortality rate ranging from 10 to 25 per cent. If competition with the chain gang did not sufficiently dampen any restive impulses in the white laborer, there was always the threat, and occasional use, of Negro strikebreakers, which did little to improve the already violent hostility of poor whites for the Negroes.

Textiles and lumber were not the whole story of Southern industrial growth, however. Railroads crept over the deltas and through the valleys. In 1890 there were some 27,000 miles in the Southern states east of the Mississippi alone—nearly as much as the whole nation had had at the outbreak of the Civil War. But half of all Southern mileage, in 1890, was already owned by 12 large companies and their affiliates. One of the largest was the Richmond and West Point Terminal Company, which controlled about 8,500 miles of Southern rail and steamship lines. It had 20 directors but 17 of them lived in New York—including two grandsons of John C. Calhoun.

Or there was the story of iron and Birmingham. Even before the Civil War,

Girls in a Virginia factory trim freshly rolled cigarettes (above) and package them (below). The experienced women could without counting pick up 20 cigarettes and pack them in neat bundles; others rolled four or five a minute. But as industrialization moved southward, James Duke's automatic cigarette-making machine was outproducing the facile women 40 to one.

sharp-eyed geologists and engineers had looked at the red hills of northern Alabama, seen that they possessed coal, iron ore and limestone, and dreamed dreams of what might happen if capital and railroads reached into the region to combine these elements. Helped along by the state government, this was done in the 1870s. Early promoters were Southerners of an adventurous bent—men like the engineer John Milner, who helped to build a railroad to an empty little spot in Jefferson County where a town named Birmingham was laid out on paper in 1871, ready for speculators in real estate. Another man, Henry De Bardeleben, was a "plunger who roved the region with the others, organizing towns and coal, iron and land companies by the dozen," in pursuance of his motto: "Life is one big game of poker."

In due time, the holdings of De Bardeleben were bought up by the better-heeled players of the Tennessee Coal, Iron and Railroad Company, financed from New York and holding sway over hundreds of thousands of acres of Southern mineral land. That was in 1892, and 15 years later the "T.C.I." itself was absorbed by the giant United States Steel Corporation, making most of Alabama's railroads and mines part of the J. P. Morgan empire. The Southern iron industry was, like so many Southern farms, absentee-owned.

The result of all this activity was a significant achievement. Between 1876 and 1901, pig-iron production increased seventeenfold in the South. And Alabama, center of the industry, by 1889 was producing more than all other Southern states put together. In 1898 Birmingham was the largest exporting point for pig iron in the country. The city, which did not exist in 1870, had a population of 26,000 in 1890. It was filled with the noise and smoke of foundries, iron furnaces and mining machinery. It also had hideous shanties, convict-labor stockades, slag heaps and company stores; a tough population, black and white; and equally tough police, who, like all other municipal officials, were highly attentive to the desires of the companies. Birmingham was, on its statistics, one of the gems of the new South. And it was a mean town.

The new South had lumber to offer for development too, and the states of the onetime Confederacy practically gave away millions of forest acres to syndicates of the '70s. Logging camps and sawmills sprang up, manned by the descendants of Indian-fighting Scotch-Irish Presbyterian pioneers or by Negroes. These laborers, whether free or convicts, worked 12 hours a day on a mush and sowbelly diet.

In sugar refineries, in turpentine distilleries and in tobacco factories which were sending out Bull Durham and Duke's Mixture to all the world—in all these places the gospel of Southern industrialism was put into action. Editors like Louisville's "Marse Henry" Watterson and Atlanta's Grady predicted dazzling accomplishments. Industrial fairs were held at frequent intervals in the cities which were the showcases of the new order—Atlanta in 1881, 1887 and 1895, Louisville in 1883, Nashville in 1897.

A NEW spirit was at work. Mark Twain noticed it when he took a trip down the lordly, lazy Mississippi of his boyhood. In places like Natchez and New Orleans he encountered men very different from the old-time planters, who lived spaciously on credit with little thought of the morrow. The new breed consisted of "brisk men, energetic of movement and speech; the dollar their god, how to get it their religion." He overheard two such men boasting of their success with margarine and "olive oil" made from cotton seed. One said:

A happy New South pays grateful attention to flirtatious Miss Textile Industries, signifying the South's campaign to attract factories. Alert Southerners saw that an agricultural economy ensured poverty. So when a preacher said, "Next to the Grace of God, what Salisbury needs is a cotton mill," people who before the war had abhorred factories shouted "Amen."

"Butter's had its *day.* . . . There's more money in oleomargarine than—why, you can't imagine the business we do. . . ." And the second boasted: "Maybe you'll butter everybody's bread pretty soon, but we'll cotton-seed his salad for him from the Gulf to Canada, that's a dead-certain thing." It was a far cry from the days when the South liked to think of itself as a reincarnation of the medieval landscapes of Sir Walter Scott.

Twain thought, on balance, that the new spirit was an improvement. Certainly there was something to admire in a South which, only a few short years after touching bottom economically and psychologically, was showing bustle and wakefulness, electric-lit and newly paved cities, and the kind of Yankee energy which the Civil War and Reconstruction had been supposed to bring to the "backward" slave states. The reality of the new South had a few things to commend it, but the reality was pitiful and shabby when compared with the wishful portraits Grady painted. He proclaimed, with fanfare, the existence of "a social system compact and closely knitted . . . a hundred farms for every plantation, fifty homes for every palace, and a diversified industry that meets the complex needs of this complex age."

The risen South showed nothing of the kind. Southern industrialization was achieved in good part at the expense of its working folk, who were thrown on the labor market as cut-rate goods to arouse the interest of out-of-town buyers. The abundant resources were only partially processed within the South's borders, and the more profitable business of turning pig iron, yard goods and raw lumber into finished goods was reserved by Northern investors for their home communities. Southern industry, it appeared, was fated merely to feed the North with materials, and Northern-dominated railroads saw to it that freight rates were raised against Southern-made commodities which threatened to violate the pattern.

Henry Watterson, barred from active service in the Civil War because of bad eyesight, served the South by editing the Tennessee "Rebel." An avid cardplayer, Watterson once gave $1,000 to his barber, another gambler. The barber lost it all the same night and then killed himself. Watterson accepted both losses philosophically: "Well," he said, "he was a good barber."

T HE profits of financing and moving Southern products, in general, did not remain in the South. Neither at the top nor the bottom of the social heap was there anything like the flush times known in the North. The South produced almost no native millionaires and industrial titans on the order of Carnegie or Vanderbilt. (One exception was James Buchanan Duke of North Carolina. The Duke family began manufacturing tobacco just after the Civil War with a single barn for a factory and a wagon to make deliveries; by 1907 young "Buck's" American Tobacco Company was a half-billion-dollar trust.) Nor was there much diffusion of whatever overflow the South caught from national prosperity. By 1900 estimated per capita wealth in the region was 50 per cent below the national level. Even this figure fails to reflect the real poverty of the South, for it includes the value of properties owned by Northern investors. Economically the South had become a colony of Northern capital.

And so the South remained. The capital which sawed Georgia pine into shingles or worked Tennessee cotton into gingham was Northern capital; the capital which built the railroads linking Southern cities was Northern; the ships which took the baled freight to and from New Orleans and Mobile, Savannah and Charleston, were Northern too. And anger stirred in the hearts of the less affluent whites who were not sharing in the glory of the new South after bearing the heat and burden of both war and Reconstruction.

The responsibility for such conditions was deeper than mere sectional villainy and the remedies more complex than a change of party at election time.

105

Yet neither responsibility nor remedy could be sought without challenges to the new South from Southerners themselves. Unfortunately, Southern political and cultural life in the years just after Reconstruction did not encourage criticism. Dissent had become near-treason. One of slavery's tragedies had been that, from about 1830 until the Civil War, it made the inquiring mind unfashionable in the South which bred Thomas Jefferson. One of Reconstruction's tragedies was that it failed to change this situation.

DEMOCRATIC voting became, after 1877, as much a mark of Southern orthodoxy as Protestantism or respect for Robert E. Lee. The real electoral battles took place in the Democratic primaries. Throughout the 1880s those clashes were generally won by men who called themselves Conservatives and who spoke up frankly for policies which, in the North, were echoed by conservatives in both major parties. These policies included hard money, assistance such as tax exemptions to railroads and industry, a free hand with the public lands for developers of natural resources and a deaf ear to the plaints of small and middling farmers. It is difficult to make general statements that will hold for all the former Confederate states over a period of some 20 years, but in the three men who dominated Georgia in the '80s was incarnated the new style in Southern politics.

The essence of this style was possession of a good Confederate war record, deprecation of one's own business connections and vilification of opponents with the charge that their candidacies—by dividing the white vote—were inviting anew the horrors of Reconstruction. John B. Gordon, Joseph E. Brown and Alfred H. Colquitt, the so-called "triumvirate," were admirably suited to this kind of campaigning. Gordon had fought valiantly for the South and was for years the commander in chief of the United Confederate Veterans. He advertised this last honor far more widely than his position as counsel of the Louisville and Nashville Railroad or his investments in insurance, publishing, mining and real estate. Gordon was Georgia's senator from 1873 to 1880 and 1891 to 1897, and its governor from 1886 to 1890.

Joseph E. Brown had been involved in both the Confederate and Reconstruction administrations of Georgia. Somehow he survived the opprobrium heaped on "scalawags," the Southerners who assisted the Republican rulers in the postwar period, and was able to retain political power. As president of the Western and Atlantic Railroad, the Southern Railway and Steamship Company, the Walker Coal and Iron Company and the Dade Coal Company, he was also forgiven his apostasy of refusing to relinquish control of Georgia's troops to Jefferson Davis during the war. Brown, like Gordon, served as senator for more than a decade. The third man, Colquitt, was a large-scale landholder who lent the social attractions of the planter class to the trio, but also invested in textiles, mining and fertilizer manufacture. As governor he did nothing to disturb these interests.

Elsewhere in the South, from Virginia to Texas, the men who won Democratic primaries were closely associated with the companies in the van of Southern commercial development. Inevitably they pursued policies that closely resembled those of the hated Republicans of Reconstruction days. Public lands rich in minerals and timber were sold for pennies an acre. Taxes on industrial property were lightened and restrictions on corporations were unthought of. When the time came for appropriations for rural roads, public

In Texas, convicts chop logs while guards keep close watch. Because so many of the South's men had been lost in the war, laborers were in great demand—so great, in fact, that common vagrants might be paired with murderers on the chain gangs. But gang work was so horrible that men often tried to escape the work by cutting arm and leg tendons or by breaking their legs.

schools and welfare services, state cupboards were bare. All such services were cut to the bone; the tax burden, even though reduced, fell chiefly on hard-pressed landowners. As a result illiteracy, as well as poverty, continued to distinguish the Southern back country.

The Bourbons, so-called, who ran these administrations kept a tight rein over their states by an iron control of the party machinery. Often they inherited machines neatly developed by the Reconstruction governments, which had concentrated the appointment of hundreds of local officials—particularly those who counted votes—in the hands of the governors. Various dissenters who tried to break through—spokesmen for free silver or for more extensive programs of agricultural and industrial education—were thrown back in most cases. Ominously, the Negro often was used as an instrument of the Bourbons in beating off these independents.

There were at least two ways in which this was done. In the first place, so long as Negroes continued to vote in the South after the Civil War—and they did—some of them adhered to a skeleton Republican party organization. The Democratic bosses kept such mortuary remnants of Reconstruction in prominent public view as a reminder to voters that the official Democratic slate was the chosen agent of the white men's party, and that the enemy was always ready to take advantage of any split in that party. What was more, the new Democratic leadership was able to control or buy Negro votes in order to turn the tide against insurgents. Such paternalistic conservatives as L.Q.C. Lamar of Mississippi or South Carolina's Wade Hampton could and did speak much more kindly to the Negro than the representatives of the poorer classes who saw in the ex-slave a competitor for status and the daily dollar. Negroes were given minor political posts in a number of places—were even conceded seats in the state legislatures—by the very Redeemers who had restored white supremacy in the '70s.

A small class of Negro politicians, in fact, learned to bargain between the two major parties, balancing the chances of federal patronage from the Republicans in Washington against those of Democratic gravy dispensed by the governor. These Negroes had written off Reconstruction's occasional idealism to make their compromise with the reality of white rule. The Negro was used against the white farmer in still another way. The independents and agrarian spokesmen generally came from hilly counties where slavery had never taken strong hold and the Negro population was relatively small. These hill people were consistently outvoted in the legislatures by the larger delegations of the richer and more populous counties of the black belts in which the Negroes were concentrated. Rightly or wrongly, their defeats gave the hill people an additional reason to hate the blacks of those districts.

ALL during the 1880s, therefore, the simmering white farmers of Georgia, South Carolina, Mississippi and other hard-hit Southern states got precious little help from their state governments as they fought grimly against the shackles of the crop-lien system and falling prices and rising costs of production—against the "daily defeats of crumbling barn and fence, encroaching sagebrush and erosion, and one's children growing up in illiteracy." A number of their leaders thought of appealing to the equally wretched Negro as an ally. During the '90s an attempt would be made to secure Negro co-operation. That attempt failed, and the great mass of poor whites stored up a passionate

At a North Carolina turpentine distillery, men unload casks of sap brought from the "turpentine orchards"—stands of yellow pine trees which were tapped like maple trees. The industry was North Carolina's largest, and although postwar production was almost as primitive as it had been in Revolutionary times, the state delivered two thirds of the nation's supply.

determination to get the Negro out of politics. When the leaders of the poor whites came to power as part of a fierce agrarian uprising that swept the nation, they united with the wealthy Conservatives to disfranchise the Negro. And then the Southern agrarian leaders would, in an explosion of long-suppressed frustration, pursue the Negro with the multifarious humiliations of lynch law and Jim Crow. But that is part of a later story.

M EANWHILE the South was winning, in the pages of popular magazines, the victory it had not gained on the battlefields. It was a victory that was costly to Southerners in the long run, since it blinded them to a good part of their own history. During the 1880s the major magazines of the North, most notably the *Century* (a beautifully illustrated monthly, aimed at the genteel, with an abundance of articles on noted painters, Gothic architecture and quaint rambles in foreign lands), began to run heavily to Southern materials. The *Century* ran a lengthy series of pieces on "Battles and Leaders of the Civil War," in which equal time was given to Blue and Gray alike. The *Century*, *Harper's*, the *Atlantic* and *Lippincott's*, among others, also featured Southern fiction in which a familiar pattern began to appear. Gentle and faithful old "darkies" would relate, with an appropriate comic mismanagement of the longer words, tales of how their cleverness or faithfulness had helped their beloved masters when the Yankees came.

The story almost always involved a planter family, one or more high-spirited sons, a beautiful and virtuous daughter and now and then a comic lower-class overseer. The course of true love, thwarted by family feuds or the coming of the war itself, finally ran smooth in the difficult days after the war. A Northern man might appear on the scene. If he was a scoundrel, he was soon dismissed, but in many cases he was one of the "better sort." He recognized the gallantry of the South, chuckled at the antics of the darkies and made it clear that *he*, at least, knew that it was only right that the South had been restored to the proper white upper-class hands.

Sometimes the converted Yankee was rewarded with the hand of the daughter, who finally consented to bury her original enmity (really a manifestation of grief for the dead Confederate lover or brother) and to marry the invader. The curtain fell on a tender embrace; the girl white and fairylike in a moonlit gown, the old black family retainer slyly peeping from the shrubbery and grinning over the approaching wedding feast.

The palm for writing of this sort went to Thomas Nelson Page, whose stories "Marse Chan" and "Meh Lady" caused hardened old Republicans, Union veterans and abolitionists from Boston to St. Louis to gulp and blow their noses. Who would not mourn when faithful Sam brought home the handsome young heir to the Channing plantation, fallen on the field of battle? And it was a cold fish indeed who would not wonder if there was not considerable truth in faithful Sam's memories of the once-execrated slavery system: "Dem wuz good ole times, marster—de bes' Sam ever see! Niggers didn' hed nothin' 'tall to do—jes' hed to 'ten' to de feedin' an' cleanin' de hosses, an' doin' what de marster tell 'em to do: an' when dey wuz sick, dey had things sent 'em out de house, an' de same doctor come to see 'em whar 'ten' to de white folks when dey wuz po'ly. Dyar warn' no trouble nor nothin'."

As a modern Southern writer put it, Southerners themselves soon came to accept this "sort of ecstatic, teary-eyed vision of the Old South as the Happy-

In 1870 the site of Birmingham, Alabama, was marked by scattered houses and cornfields. Ten years later 3,000 people lived there, most of them steelworkers like the men tending the pig-iron furnace shown above. By 1890 the population of the "magic city" had soared to over 26,000, and Birmingham had to face the challenge and the tribulation of a prospering factory town.

Happy Land." They came to believe that under slavery the only bonds the Negro had known were "those of tender understanding, trust, and loyalty." And they submerged beneath the waves of sentiment not only their view of the race problem, but their memories of all the normal social and class conflicts to which Southern flesh had been heir before 1861. The version of history they adopted was simple: everything had been better, once. There was the story of the Southern lady so carried away by the spirit of things that when a guest remarked on a gorgeous harvest moon, she exclaimed: "Oh, my, you ought to have seen that moon before the war!"

By extension, then, the men who had fought and died in defense of that prewar order were sacred. So long as the Redeemers could display their Confederate scars, they were beyond criticism. To champion labor unions, the higher criticism of the Bible or the emancipation of women—to flirt with any of these dangerous new notions—was to awaken memories of the great upheaval of 1861-1877, and to revive the dangerous, misguided idealistic Northern fallacies which had brought it on. Southern conservatism in religious and intellectual matters, born of an individualistic, frontier way of life, was reinforced by the experience of defeat. Southern fundamentalism was proverbial; a philosopher remembered growing up in a Mississippi household in which such names as "Hume, Renan, Paine, Voltaire and Darwin" belonged to "choice agents of the Prince of Darkness." Southern political rebels and Southern writers, as the 20th Century dawned, would have to break through that hard crust of conservatism and destroy the mythological Southern heritage before they could make constructive use of whatever had been the true values of the old order.

Nonetheless, the wave of moonlight-and-magnolia writing did have a strong effect in putting to a final rest the ideological ghosts of the Civil War. The reformers of the North, fighting the battles of pure government against the unwashed legions of city machine voters, lost their last vestiges of interest in the Southern Negro, who struck them now as less capable of improvement than even a two-dollar-a-vote immigrant. The Negroes, according to Edwin L. Godkin of *The Nation*, could probably never be worked into a government for which he and his fellow civil-service reformers could have much respect. Richard Watson Gilder, the *Century's* editor, observed that the Negroes "constitute a peasantry wholly untrained in, and ignorant of, those ideas of constitutional liberty and progress which are the birthright of every white voter."

In 1902, when the United States was engaged in the distasteful business of subduing the Philippines, a Tennessee-born historian was able to strike a triumphant note: "The Republican party, in . . . imposing the sovereignty of the United States upon eight millions of Asiatics, has changed its view in regard to the political relations of races and has at last virtually accepted the ideas of the South upon that subject."

WITH the South accepting the coming of industry, and the North burying opposition to the white Southerner's demand for absolute political supremacy, nothing stood in the way of an emotional peacemaking. Veterans at joint Union-Confederate reunions shook hands and buried the hatchet. A Republican author of a volume of recollections of Lincoln wrote in 1891, "Sectional differences in our republic belong to the past." Jefferson Davis, in his last speech, given in 1888, had made the same point. Now, however, it was official.

To provide fuel for Birmingham's blast furnaces, a row of hungry coke ovens devours trainloads of coal. The heavy demands for coal and the need to transport ingots of pig iron to market brought six railroads converging on Birmingham. "Harper's Weekly" called the city "one of the chief glories of the New South, and a source of admiring wonder to the whole country."

Lucius Quintus Cincinnatus Lamar, Southern minister to Russia, "gorge[d] himself with work" despite ill health. (He had apoplexy, vertigo and kidney ailments.) In London during the war he propagandized for the South and once described Negroes as "not attaining . . . to the civilization of a fig leaf."

General John Brown Gordon, a postwar senator from Georgia, has been described as the "most important military figure in the history of Georgia." Gordon was so eloquent a speaker that one soldier pleaded with him to stop prebattle talks, for the general "makes me feel like I could storm Hell."

By the end of the 1880s it was clear that the industrializing of the South, which had been the economic program of Reconstruction, was continuing under new management. The idealistic side of Reconstruction—the providing of a democratic, equal way of life for Negro and white—was dead. The Negro had little opportunity to express his discontent. Economically he was a near serf. Politically he had been silenced. Socially he was an outcast. He had been aided by a number of philanthropic and educational foundations financed by both the North and South and often led by high-minded Southerners who, if they still held the Negro to be an inferior, at least had a sense of fairness and responsibility. Now Negro leadership began tentatively to emerge and it was fitting that a Negro should pronounce the official death notice on Reconstruction ideals, and that he should do so in Atlanta, at an industrial exposition held to glorify the new South.

THE man was a remarkable American of the Gilded Age, Booker Taliaferro Washington. He was born in a slave cabin in Virginia in 1856. As a boy he starved and sweated at a succession of backbreaking menial jobs, knew misery and dirt from the skin out. He picked up some education in the household of a New England woman where he worked as a servant, then applied for admission to the Hampton Institute. This was a vocational and teachers' training school for Negroes founded in 1868, in the flush of Reconstruction's plans for uplifting the Negro, by General Samuel C. Armstrong, the Hawaiian-born son of Yankee missionaries. Washington worked his way through Hampton as a janitor. From his New England mentors he absorbed all the Calvinist virtues—cleanliness, hard work, thrift, perseverance.

After a period of teaching in Negro institutions, Washington came to Tuskegee in Alabama, to start a training school for Negro teachers. As principal of the Tuskegee Institute, he worked tirelessly to expand its facilities for industrial training. A vision was opened to him, of a population of Southern Negroes schooled in habits of self-discipline and cleanliness and skilled in such crafts as blacksmithing, harness making, brickmaking and metalwork. Would there not, somehow, be room and acceptance in the new South for so productive a people? Washington thought so, and with incredible energy and persuasiveness set about convincing Northern and Southern philanthropists that donations to Tuskegee would help to bless a progressive South with a trained Negro labor force.

By 1895 he had enough of a reputation throughout the country to win an invitation to speak at the opening of the Cotton States and International Exposition in Atlanta. Washington's address created the kind of storm there that Henry Grady's had in New York nearly nine years before. He launched into an eloquent plea for an end to the agitation of questions of social equality. The Negro's best friends, said Washington, were those white men of the South who gave him "a man's chance in the commercial world." Let the South rely on the "most patient, faithful, law-abiding and unresentful people that the world has seen." They would then, Washington promised, "buy your surplus land, make blossom the waste places in your fields, and run your factories." Let the Negro in turn worry less about his privileges and more about his preparation for exercising the privileges. "The opportunity to earn a dollar in a factory" was worth more than the opportunity to spend one in an opera house. Let both races be, he summed up, "in all things . . . purely social" as separate as the fingers of the hand, "yet as the hand in all things essential to mutual progress."

The crowds cheered; the governor of Georgia pressed across the platform to shake Washington's hand. He was launched on a career as the spokesman for the Negro race which would make him a front-page figure wherever he went, and until his death in 1915, a welcome visitor in the homes and offices of the mighty of the earth. What he had done, without mentioning politics, was to offer to use his leadership to withdraw the Negro from politics; to gamble that the white man who would not concede social equality would, in sheer self-interest, lend a hand in increasing the producing, earning and purchasing power of the Negro who constituted one third of the Southern population. The Negro would forego social (and political) opportunities in return for a fair share in economic progress. The solution—if solution it was— spelled yet another delay in the facing of post-Reconstruction problems.

Critics since 1895 have accused Washington of a surrender to the forces of white supremacy. They point out that the condition of the Negro grew worse, rather than better, after the compromise, and that Washington's emphasis on preparing the Negro for craftsmanship and small-business ownership took no account of the changing industrial scene, the onset of the assembly line or the giant corporation. Defenders have argued that Washington did the only thing possible; that the lynching rate was on the rise, segregation laws multiplying and Southern states already in the process of disfranchising Negroes when he spoke at Atlanta. They claim that Washington was making the best of an impossible situation and that economic self-sufficiency would have to precede effective political action.

Both schools miss a significant point. Whether Washington spoke correctly or wisely for the Negro or not, he spoke precisely with the voice of the white advocates of the new South and of the Northern spokesmen of the gospel of self-help. He, too, saw the progress of the nation and of his race as something to be measured in production statistics. He had gone from rags to solid respectability by frequent washing, infrequent rests and a resistance to anything impractical. (Until his death he rarely took a vacation, almost never read a novel, abhorred the sight of a speck of dirt on wall or floor.) He felt that Negroes were foolish to try to be artists, preachers or full-time politicians. If Negroes could become the economic and cultural counterparts of the American middle class of the 1890s, he felt, American life could not long shut the door on them.

Washington's speech was a perfect companion piece to Grady's, a perfect gem of the new order that had alike swept aside the old, agrarian South and the old, crusading North. Both John C. Calhoun and William Lloyd Garrison were now of the past, firmly and forever.

THUS the South marched along with the new era—somewhat haltingly and awkwardly, looking back now and then and hiding a few rips in its garments. Like the West, it was a tributary of the North; unlike the West, its dominant mood was nostalgia instead of unrestricted future-worship. As of 1890, the South had postponed the solution of many of its most urgent problems. In this way as much as in any other, perhaps, it showed its restored unity with the nation. It was to remain at one with the nation in weathering the storms of the 1890s.

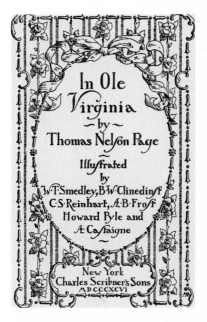

Thomas Page, though only eight at the outbreak of the Civil War, memorialized ante-bellum life. His romantic stories, such as "In Ole Virginia" (above), with their tender illustrations of Southern belles and their suitors (below), gave a defeated people an arm to lean on through the hard postwar years.

111

With Mississippi channels clogged, only a few ships are berthed at New Orleans in 1873. But work was soon under way to deepen the river.

The rebirth of a gallant city

UNTIL the latter part of the 19th Century, New Orleans, the city of Mardi Gras and gaiety, had a history of dizzying ups and downs. It was founded by the French in the early 1700s, but in 1764 its residents were dismayed to learn that their city had been surreptitiously handed over to the Spaniards. In the next four decades, there were two more changes of allegiance; the city was returned to France and then conveyed to the United States as part of Jefferson's Louisiana Purchase. With the coming of the Civil War, New Orleans was firmly in the Confederate camp. But the gateway to the Mississippi was too important a prize, and Union forces under Admiral Farragut seized it in 1862. The tribulations of defeat, occupation and Reconstruction are still remembered. Everywhere there was corruption that crossed party, color and sectional lines. Poverty, broken levees and spoiled crops added to the misery. Worst of all, the Mississippi was clogged with silt, and river traffic, the lifeblood of New Orleans, dwindled to a trickle.

In the 1870s, the business community made an attempt at biracial cooperation (including remarkably successful integrated public schools) that foundered on mutual race hostility. The Democratic politicians ousted the city government made up of a coalition anathema to many ex-Rebels. Restored to power, the Democrats used various combinations of federal, state and local funds to further an overdue public works program, notably including a system of silt-catching jetties. Though corruption and a festering racial problem persisted, economic conditions improved in the 1880s, and the "Crescent City" proved a very colorful lady, as the pictures on the following pages illustrate.

A LOVE OF PAGEANTRY draws a noble muster in 1872 for the 35th annual New Orleans Volunteer Firemen's Parade. This painting is a pictorial who's who of New Orleans and shows the portraits of most of the prominent citizens in their firemen's uniforms. Though Federal occupation had another five years to run, the city was already astir with new hope and vigor.

A lush, primeval land of watery wilderness

IN ages long past, the waters of the Gulf of Mexico lapped over much of what is now Louisiana. Then silt, brought down the valley by the Mississippi, slowly created a sprawling, swampy country with the languorous bayous, teeming with birds and fur-bearing animals, that became an unmistakable hallmark of the Mississippi Delta region *(opposite)*. Every year floods spread over the land, leaving behind rich deposits of alluvial soil which later proved hospitable to the growing of cotton, sugar and rice. The soil's inherent wealth, coupled with a long growing season and the introduction of the slave labor system, gave rise to vast and luxuriant plantations in the area around New Orleans *(above)*. When Northern victory in the Civil War brought abolition, the Delta planter lost his life-and-death control over his chattel manpower. Faced with ruin, these estates had to turn their acreage to sharecropping, and the era of graceful living on plantations was doomed.

A RICH MANSION called Bon Séjour, or "Good Stopping Place," sumptuously draws the eye down an avenue of huge live oaks. Bon Séjour was the crowning jewel of an ante-bellum estate near New Orleans. Similar plantations at times ran to 10,000 acres.

A QUIET BAYOU in the southern Mississippi Delta *(right)* wends its meandering way through a sprawling cypress swamp. New Orleans itself is built on such low-lying land. In some places the water level is so close to the surface that houses have no cellars.

A ROUGH CABIN used by a trapper sits at the edge of the Mississippi. The region around New Orleans teemed with muskrat, raccoon and mink; and fur trappers—using dugout boats *(center)* to gather their catches—learned every foot of the landscape.

AN APPLE VENDOR noisily peddles his wares to a Creole matron. Her servant watches.

The famed French Quarter's heritage of another era

I N New Orleans the term "Creole" has always been a badge of distinction. It applies to native-born descendants of the original French and Spanish settlers —the old-line upper crust. Quite early in the city's history, the Creoles built themselves picturesque homes around courtyards which reflected their Mediterranean heritage *(right)*. Generations of Creoles lived a traditionally French life in the section called the Vieux Carré—literally, the "old square." But like all seaports, New Orleans had its disreputable side. Certain streets of the Vieux Carré became the center of raffish night life. And the Creole elite found itself sharing the quarter with more than 1,000 prostitutes and perhaps three times that many purveyors of food, drink and music.

THE OLD ABSINTHE HOUSE, built in 1805 and named for the lethal beverage served here, is quiescent in this daylight study. But at night it was a hub of revelry in the sporting district.

This old Creole-quarter house is characterized by a stucco exterior,

THE FRENCH MARKET is little more than a roofed shelter. In this primitive forerunner of the supermarket, the enterprising merchants stocked all the many and exotic delicacies demanded by the Creole *bons vivants*.

A VIEUX CARRE COURTYARD reveals the serene and inward-looking characteristics of most Creole homes. Drab and shuttered from the street side, the houses concealed airy enclosures alive with fountains and flowering plants.

a tile roof and, inevitably, a wrought-iron balcony.

K.O.M CARNIVAL EDITION KNIGHTS

The Picayune

1887 FEBRUARY 17th

NEW ORLEANS, LA.

LITHOGRAPHD BY T. FITZWILLIAM & Co. NEW ORLEANS.

No. 1

The imagination and skill used in preparing floats for the Mardi Gras parade are seen in these drawings of elaborate entries for the parade

FANCIFUL COSTUMES for the 1882 Proteus krewe parade are supposed to embody Egyptian motifs, but they have an Indian look.

Floats created by the Momus krewe for the 1884 Mardi Gras pageant illustrate aspects of "The Passions," the flamboyant topic chosen for

No. 3—JEALOUSY—Amestris.

No. 4—REVENGE—The Death of Caligula.

of 1887. The theme chosen for that year's spectacle was "Myths of the New World." The sketches appeared in the New Orleans "Picayune."

The imaginative gaiety of Fat Tuesday

IN French, Mardi Gras means Fat Tuesday, the Tuesday before Lent begins, and New Orleans has been celebrating Fat Tuesday ever since the earliest settlers brought over the tradition from France. Though the first organized parade was held in 1837, it was not until the 1870s and '80s that the New Orleans Mardi Gras really hit its stride. That period saw the formation of some of the most famous "krewes," or secret societies, which sponsored the parades and balls, all collectively called Carnival. Since each of the krewes held its own celebration, the effect was to introduce an element of friendly rivalry. Competition ultimately became so keen that a krewe's parade and its ensuing ball were a year in preparation, what with building suitable floats *(above and below)* and making elaborate costumes *(opposite)*, all in accordance with a chosen theme. The whole city, of course, delighted in the festivities. But the great balls afterward were as ultraexclusive as each of the krewes could make them. Weeks were spent narrowing down the lists of those lucky enough to be favored with one of the difficult-to-counterfeit invitations *(right)*.

ELABORATE INVITATION for the 1890 Rex ball is a garishly filigreed fan. A limited number were issued. Once, a $2,000 reward offer failed to get back two missing invitations.

that year's cavalcade. Some of these colorful New Orleans parades featured as many as 15 of these carefully built, horse-drawn displays.

No. 6—GLUTTONY—The Banquet of Vitellius.

No. 7—ENVY—Saul and David.

A PROUD NEGRO WOMAN wears a bright turbanlike *tignon*, the one-time compulsory badge for a woman of mixed blood. Although the Spaniards meant this as a discriminatory sign, the women defeated them by making the *tignon* a beautiful hat.

A HECTIC DANCE to the music of an accordion *(right)* is an abandoned expression of joy with voodoo overtones. Such dances were a Negro tradition even in slave times, but in the 1880s they became so orgiastic the city fathers called a halt.

The lasting fruits of an easygoing way of life

REVELRY ignored the color line in the New Orleans of the late 1800s. To be sure, the Negro played no significant part in the formal pageantry of the Mardi Gras. But he had his own diversions *(above)*, and they were every bit as gay—and considerably more frequent. It was a spontaneous sort of gaiety and doubtless stemmed from the uniquely generous attitude toward the Negro which had always prevailed in New Orleans. In prewar days, a slave unquestionably had been a slave; but freedom was easier to attain than in other parts of the South. Not a few Creole gentlemen kept mulatto or quadroon mistresses, and children born of such relation-

ships were at times sent to Europe by their fathers to get the education denied them at home. To a great many New Orleans slaveowners, the Negro was more than just a piece of property. He had an identity and he could call his soul his own. If he chose to practice voodoo discreetly *(left, above)*, it was pretty much his own affair. This climate of friendly tolerance did not survive Reconstruction, for the rancor of defeat was expressed in a determination "to keep the Negro in his place." But the Negro continued to express himself. In time he created his own idiomatic music, which was finally "discovered" in New Orleans and which we now refer to as jazz.

A COURTED NEGRO is the central figure in this caricature disparaging the short-lived Independent Party which tried for Negro support during Reconstruction.

THE COTTON MARKET in New Orleans is seen in this 1873 painting by the French artist Edgar Degas. "Factors," who were both moneylenders and sales agents, examine and grade samples (on table) of the new crop. As bankers, factors charged planters up to 30 per cent interest; as agents, they got 2.5 per cent of sales. In either case the fees were unconscionable.

Recovery founded on the wealth in the soil

IN the economic wreckage left by the Civil War, few Southern states had more obstacles to overcome than Louisiana. Between 1868 and 1875, free-spending carpetbaggers tripled the state's debt to more than $50 million; this in turn so increased New Orleans rates that the sheriff made some 47,000 tax seizures from 1871 to 1873. The old plantation system had been doomed by the ending of slave labor; oppressive taxation speeded the process. Louisiana was busy the last quarter of the 19th Century trying to regain its former prosperity. Adjusting to new conditions, some plantations were shifted to a sharecropping basis; others were taken over by Northern financiers. Slowly shipments of cotton and sugar began coming down the Mississippi. New Orleans fared somewhat better in spite of widespread municipal graft and corruption and the presence of troops, which occupied the city until 1877. The Port of New Orleans resumed its function as a transshipment point. By 1880 Southern cotton production had surpassed the prewar production levels, and about one third of this all-important crop was bought and sold at New Orleans (left).

A SUGAR REFINERY adjoins cane fields near New Orleans. A major postwar crop, sugar later suffered because of soil problems and competition.

Boom times for the riverman

Inky pitch-pine smoke (the signal of imminent departure) billows from the lofty stacks of steamboats loading at New Orleans. All the staples of the South await shipment—bags of rice, molasses and sugar in casks, lumber, and of course cotton. The side-wheeler *Natchez (left background)* may be the same

Natchez (there were several so named) which raced upstream in 1870 and established the record of 3 days 18 hours 14 minutes to St. Louis. For better than 50 years, the activity shown here brought wealth to New Orleans. At times these "swimming volcanoes," as steamboats were once called, crowded the shoreline three deep for a distance of five miles. However, by 1883, when William Walker painted this scene, the railroads were siphoning off more and more freight traffic and the era of the Mississippi steamboat was waning. But by then the city's prosperity was no longer so heavily dependent on the river.

125

6. THE RISE OF THE TRUST

THE term "monopoly" was a fighting word to the American public in the 1870s and 1880s. Tariff reformers, currency reformers, farm spokesmen, labor organizers and dissenters of every size and pattern used the term to describe some kind of faceless evil that threatened the republic's virtue and freedom. To economists, uninterested in the emotional effect of words, the term was distressingly imprecise. Monopoly—"the exclusive control of the supply of any commodity or service in a given market"—was rare then, as it has been rare at any time in the history of the United States.

A factual description of the state of business enterprise in the nation after the Civil War required the drier terms found in the lexicon of political economy. Briefly, then, machinery reduced production costs and expansion opened new markets. Profits rose. New entrepreneurs were attracted into the field, competed vigorously with each other, produced a surplus and, under the necessities of business warfare, slashed prices. Profits fell. There was then a general mortality among marginal firms—those that could not push their costs of production down beneath new low prices. Finally, the assets of the deceased organizations were taken over by a reduced number of survivors. Competition had yielded concentration as one of its fruits.

Such a description is far too simplified for the purposes of a modern economist. It would have been regarded as far too dispassionate by antimonopoly crusaders of the '80s—and, surprisingly, by businessmen as well. For if the

GIANT CORPORATIONS are attacked as "the bosses of the Senate" in an 1889 cartoon. The next year, to curb their power, Congress approved the Sherman Antitrust Act.

127

reformer would have missed the brimstone aroma of villainy, the man of the market place would have found that the mere word "competition" gave no hint of the intensity of his struggle to keep his business alive.

The kind of feeling that competition aroused in some men was best conveyed in letters like one written by a Michigan lumber merchant, Henry H. Crapo, during the depression of 1857 to 1858. "Every man for the last few years who has had a 40-acre lot of pine land and could raise three shillings of cash and the 'balance' on 'Bond and Mortgage' has built a saw mill somewhere and commenced sawing lumber—and has then sold it for just what it would bring, without any reference to the cost of manufacture. . . . This class of men . . . have not only fouled their own nests but have prostrated and crippled the business by their unreasonable competition, with which the solvent and judicious and prudent manufacturer has had to contend."

And 30 years later, little had changed in the economic scene. In 1888 the vice president of the National Millers' Association lamented to his colleagues that even in a business which was "always in fashion," the preparation of bread, "ambition has overreached . . . discretion and judgment . . . the commercial triumph of former seasons had to be surpassed by still more dazzling figures. As our glory increased our profits became smaller, until now the question is not how to surpass the record, but how to maintain our position and how to secure what we have in our possession."

It was not surprising that harassed businessmen, battling over markets not yet fully developed and struggling simultaneously to pump money into expansion and pay dividends to attract fresh capital, should yearn to bring order into chaos. They decided that competing units had to be banded together by combination to present a united front to raw material suppliers and transportation agents, to hold production to sensible limits and maintain prices at reasonable levels, to divide territories among an efficient number of producers. The economic causes and consequences of combination were then (and still are) the subject of debate; the details difficult to explain by any neat theory; the social and political effects shot with controversy. Regardless of the debate, combination and growth continued.

Combination took the form not only of unifying firms within an industry, but also of sweeping all the factors in a productive process—for example, from raw iron ore to finished tenpenny nails—under a single control. Thus, while combination was an escape from destructive competition, it was also a means of growth. The growth of the consolidation movement is best visible in the story of rails, steel and oil. These key industries in the creation of a modern economy furnished the pattern for similar action in communications, in sugar and tobacco processing, and elsewhere. But the critics of combination saved their most vigorous diatribes for the rail, steel and oil combinations, whose captains and kings still bestride the popular history of the period, whether as "robber barons" or "statesmen of industry."

F EW industries went through the roaring cycle of expansion, competition and consolidation as swiftly as the railroads. With new mileage running into the thousands every year of the '70s and '80s, shippers of freight found themselves the happy choosers of a variety of routes and rates. In the late '70s, for instance, there were 20 competitive routes between St. Louis and Atlanta (varying in length from 526 to 1,855 miles, thanks to various detours

Jim Fisk, caricatured as "The Barnum of Wall Street," balances his unsteady enterprises with aplomb. The engine signifies the Erie Railroad, which he and his associate, Jay Gould, controlled. The Fisk-maintained ballet company is on his right arm and a militia regiment perches on his left. Fisk's true forte was finance—he was "first in the pockets of his countrymen."

and meandering routings. These alternatives to a direct route might have been roundabout, but they were unquestionably competitive.

The trouble was that the rates would not stay put, and the shipper who snapped at a bargain rate often found that a week or two of delay might have brought another freight reduction worth thousands to him. On the other hand, if he waited a week too long, the price of transportation might surge upward and wipe out the profit on a transaction that had temporarily tied up his entire capital.

WHILE this chaos of rate and route gave combination its opportunity, cutthroat competition was not the only spur to combination. Sometimes consolidation was indispensable to the creation of a route that could provide traffic sufficient to meet expenses and produce a fair return for investors. (It should be remembered that the average cost of transportation declined rapidly all through this period.) Combination was also used by unscrupulous operators interested only in defrauding the stockholders, plundering assets or manipulating stock prices. The motives for consolidation—good, evil or mixed —varied. What was constant was the thrust toward merger.

The classic pattern of consolidation saw the lesser fish swallowed by the greater. By 1895 the four great trunk lines between the Atlantic coast and Chicago (the New York Central, Pennsylvania, Erie and Baltimore & Ohio) had integrated into their systems dozens of smaller lines whose names reflected the dreams of promoters who expected their towns to become mighty marts of trade—the Pittsburgh, Fort Wayne and Chicago, the Marietta and Cincinnati, the Terre Haute and Indianapolis.

It was in the great West, however, that consolidation had the kind of scope appropriate to the terrain. In 1872, freebooting Jay Gould abandoned the Erie Railroad, which he, Jim Fisk and Daniel Drew had gutted, for the broader opportunities across the Mississippi. Within nine years, Gould was riding high, wide and handsome as the master of a railroad kingdom in which Denver, St. Louis and Kansas City were key towns.

In California, in the '80s, the words "railroad" and "monopoly" had become virtually synonymous with each other and with the names of the "Big Four"— Leland Stanford, Charles Crocker, Mark Hopkins and Collis P. Huntington —and their Southern Pacific system.

Transportation in the Northwest, by 1881, was largely in the hands of a onetime German immigrant boy named Henry Villard, but his control was soon challenged by James J. Hill, the vigorous boss of the Great Northern. Five major lines, all rooted in Chicago—the Illinois Central, the Burlington, the Milwaukee, the North Western and the Rock Island—dominated traffic in the north central states by 1890.

Concentrated ownerships such as these were one way of reducing strife among individual roads. Another was to combine in pools or gentlemen's agreements, in which rates were stabilized, traffic prorated among the warring lines and revenues politely divided up at given periods. The pools had one major drawback for the railroad owners themselves: it was difficult to get genuine agreement on what constituted a fair basis for profitable rates on different lines. And, once consensus was secured, there was no way to police the arrangement if some members grew unco-operative at cake-cutting time.

Consolidation and pools spared the economy the agonies of price war, but

Daniel Drew donates money to the religious school he helped to found (now Drew University). Starting as a livestock drover, the "Deacon" made an immense fortune only to be ruined by his partners, Jim Fisk and Jay Gould. When under stress Drew would alternate wildly between piety and intemperance, ending up at fervent prayer or in a hotel room for a long drunk.

producers and shippers soon discovered that they were not always better off when railroads did *not* compete. To begin with, noncompeting roads set rate schedules that were high enough to make up for previous losses. Secondly, individual systems or pooled roads that faced competition on some of their routes imposed unreasonably high rates on customers in other areas where there was no competition. This was the source of the notorious discrimination between towns and between entire regions, and of the "short-haul" versus "long-haul" rate classifications.

Just as the railroads discriminated between places, so they dispensed favors among shippers with thorough partiality. Favored shippers got secret rebates, preferential (and money-saving) freight classification and false weighing. In return, the shippers promised to use no other railroad or land or water route. Both sides were happy: the manufacturer could undersell and squeeze out competitors, while the lines had a new weapon to destroy other forms of transportation.

Railroad men defended these practices. As the president of one line put it: The producer of transportation, like the producer of other commodities, should be free to sell for all he can get and to make different prices to different persons if necessary. The country, however, was coming to think otherwise by the '70s.

Suddenly America was facing a paradox not thought of in the happy days of the '50s and '60s when the iron horse was the key to a glorious future. Competitive railroading—if such a thing were possible—was wasteful, chaotic, unsettling. Noncompetitive railroading, on the other hand, vested in corporation officers awesome powers of life or death over individuals, cities and whole regions, and put authority greater than that of governors, lawmakers and judges in the possession of railroad directors who were responsible to no popular electorate, governed by no constitution.

The nation protested and pondered. Then it moved slowly, over constitutional and emotional barriers, toward the unfamiliar device of regulation, unaware as yet of the new problems that regulation would bring. Inseparable from the protest against railroad abuses was the anger generated by the development of other giant concentrations such as the steel industry.

THE surge of railroad building in the '80s called for immense quantities of steel rails. As they supplied this demand, the mills were being drawn into a closer organization. The census of 1880 had shown 1,005 different plants engaged in steelmaking, but the bulk of production was coming increasingly from large plants like Carnegie's J. Edgar Thomson works or the furnaces of Carnegie's major competitors.

In 1883 Carnegie's firm bought control of the H.C. Frick Coke Company. Frick, the slight, pale grandson of a famous distiller, had spent years quietly buying valuable mining properties. These produced the best coke in the country—and coke was indispensable to steelmaking. Frick hated waste, competition and labor unions with equal zeal. Now his efforts were to be directed to the greater glory of Carnegie Brothers & Company, Limited, which continued to expand by absorbing rival works.

Other giants were emerging in steel. The Colorado Coal and Iron Company put up its first Bessemer mill in 1882 to roll rails for the new lines beginning to pierce the Rockies. While it suffered from Eastern competition, it had

Tobacco-chewing George Hearst was one of the few popular mining millionaires. "Uncle George" would stroll through San Francisco with a bag of gold pieces which he slipped to needy sourdoughs. When his son, William Randolph, asked for ice cream for his playmates, he handed little Willie $20.

Unlike the usual unlettered prospector, William A. Clark studied at the Columbia School of Mines to aid him in staking claims. His real start toward his copper fortune came from a 500-mile horseback trip in sub-zero temperatures, to bring in tobacco which he sold to isolated miners at an $8,000 profit.

sufficient health by 1892 to reorganize as Colorado Fuel and Iron, with a $13 million capitalization covering 15 mines, 800 coke ovens, three blast furnaces and other assets.

These mighty corporations were just on the verge of bigger and better expansion. What was more, they were extending their control over the steps in the fabrication of steel. In the '90s, Carnegie's company included Minnesota ore ranges, a fleet of Great Lakes ore boats and a railroad network that connected the lake ports to its Pennsylvania furnaces.

The increasing size of the steel companies brought little reduction in competition—in direct contrast to the situation that prevailed in railroading. Expansion in steel, whether of an operating firm like Carnegie's or by the J. P. Morgan-created combination called the Federal Steel Company, was primarily for technological efficiency. The competitive struggle among the great steel complexes continued to be fierce.

Strong man of the Great Northern Railroad, Jim Hill lost the sight of his left eye as a child. His good eye could blaze "like a living coal" when he was in a rage, giving him such a saturnine expression that children sang: "'Twixt Hill and Hell, there's just one letter / Were Hill in Hell, we'd feel much better."

PEOPLE would later talk of the steel trust or its fellow trusts in cordage, biscuits, electric equipment, tin plate or packed meat. Yet the term "trust" itself—meaning any combination which reduced competition—was first brought into public notice in 1882, when a lawyer for the Standard Oil Company of Ohio set up a simple-looking agreement whereby the stockholders of that corporation (and a number of others subsidiary to or allied with it) transferred their properties to a board of nine trustees.

The transaction sounded innocuous enough, but it was done for the benefit of a company that was already the feared and admired ruler of the oil-refining business. If the word "trust" described Standard Oil, the very image of near-monopoly power, then it described any business colossus that could dictate to competitors, customers, railroads and lawmakers.

Standard Oil was the creation of John Davison Rockefeller, a slender young man who came out of the western New York region that produced so many business leaders in the 19th Century. Rockefeller's father was a patent-medicine salesman, his mother a tight-lipped daughter of Scots, who was loving, but unsparing of the rod. She taught her children such useful maxims as "Willful waste makes woeful want"—something that Rockefeller never forgot. He was one of a generation of young men who grew up to believe that there was little life outside of business, and no goals in business outside of bigness and success, which were synonymous. His own and later eras spent much time in debating whether John D. Rockefeller was a good or a bad man. His contemporaries, friends and enemies alike, agreed on his extraordinary single-mindedness in the pursuit of profit—legitimate profit, certainly, and profit which was tithed and more than tithed for charity from the start, but steadily accumulating profit.

Austere Collis P. Huntington, a director of the Southern Pacific Railroad, at 63 married his second wife. She convinced him that he ought to enjoy his wealth. Together they sampled antiques and the opera. Late in life he was thought of as "a hard and cheery old man, with no more soul than a shark."

As a small boy, Rockefeller earned his first money by outwitting a hen turkey that was hiding her eggs. As a reward, he was given the privilege of raising and selling the chicks. When he was 12, he made his first loan out of his own savings—$50 at 7 per cent—and discovered, as one biographer puts it, that "capital earned money more easily than muscle did." The family moved to Ohio in 1853 when he was 14. Rockefeller, boarding in Cleveland, worked hard in high school, practiced piano, attended the Erie Street Baptist Church and listened gravely to his father's lessons in business sagacity. He seemed an average young man, but more than usually serious, thoughtful, pious and frugal. One of his sisters was shrewd enough to guess the direction of his thoughts. "When it's raining porridge," she said, "you'll find John's dish right side up."

In 1855 Rockefeller got his first job with the firm of Hewitt and Tuttle, commission merchants and produce shippers, and found "all the method and system of the office . . . delightful." He earned $50 for his first three months of work. Four years later, he and a partner, Maurice Clark, went into the same business. In 1863, in a momentous day for American business history, he persuaded Clark to join him and Samuel Andrews, a young chemist, in a new venture—petroleum refining. The flood of Pennsylvania crude oil was beginning to pour into Cleveland, among other places, and the prospects of a future in the business seemed enticing.

At least they did to Rockefeller, but Clark moved reluctantly and plainly meant to keep most of his eggs in the wholesale produce business basket. So in 1865 Rockefeller borrowed enough to buy Clark's share of the refining enterprise, and the firm of Rockefeller and Andrews appeared on the scene to do battle with about 30 other Cleveland refineries. That was the nucleus of Standard Oil, though the company was not reorganized and incorporated under that name until 1870. By then, already operating on a large scale, Rockefeller was trying to rationalize and control a petroleum industry that was as wide open, unpredictable, lavish and dangerous as the hell-raising shantytowns of the oil fields themselves. Everyone in the business was something of a wildcat, but now the tamer had arrived.

When it took its new name, the Standard Oil Company was capitalized at one million dollars. Among its assets were a New York export sales office, two refineries, a barrelmaking plant, tank cars, warehouses, timberlands and docking facilities at Great Lakes ports. Although Standard was the largest single oil manufactory in the world, it was still relatively easy to enter the refining business. The supply of raw materials was dependent on luck and subject to violent fluctuations, the tendency to overproduce irresistible; prices were as zigzag as a worm fence.

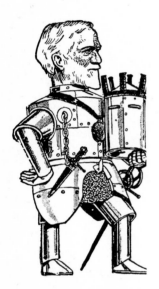

Garbed as a white knight, Andrew Carnegie stands in the product of his mills. When he turned to charity, he gave even to groups to which he was apathetic. Though not a churchgoer, he gave pipe organs to many churches to develop "a taste for good music." On Sundays he liked to float in his swimming pool "while a Highlander . . . plays sacred music on his pipes."

THE all-important mission of Standard, as Rockefeller saw it, would be to drive out unpredictable competitors (perhaps he did not see that this could ultimately mean *all* competitors) in order to regularize matters. To this end he moved to make his own business as efficient as possible and to undersell rivals by achieving reductions in the cost of production through good management. He also made use of the power of the railroads to force out the "irregulars."

Standard had already received rebates on its oil shipments from the major lines serving Cleveland. Late in 1871, however, Standard joined with several independents in a secret refiners' pool, known as the South Improvement Company, which signed contracts with the three trunk-line railroads, the Pennsylvania, the New York Central and the Erie, promising them regular and evenly prorated oil traffic. In return, the insiders in the South Improvement scheme would receive rebates on their own oil shipments, rebates on their *competitors'* shipments and full information on competitors' consignments—where from, to whom and at what valuation. No independent refinery could hope to fight such a powerful combine.

The plan was revealed shortly after its birth and stirred up such violent reaction that it was dropped. It now appears that Standard did not originate the idea. But by an interesting coincidence, during three spring months of 1872 Standard was suddenly enabled to buy out no fewer than 21 of the other 26 refineries in Cleveland. There seems little doubt that Rockefeller was able to hold his favored position with the railroads as a club over his rivals. The question was: what would he do next?

One refiner, Isaac Hewitt, later testified before an investigating committee that after Rockefeller approached him he went to the New York Central for advice and was told: "You better sell—you better get clear—better sell out—no help for it." Sell out he did, for Standard Oil stock. So did men like Frank Arter, Oliver Payne, Joseph Stanley and many others who had once dreamed, perhaps, of being oil kings themselves. Their Standard stock made some of them wealthy, but by 1872 they were vassals of the liege lord of oildom, the 33-year-old Rockefeller. Standard was shipping 10,000 barrels a day and was in control of one fourth the country's refining capacity. It was time for bigger things.

THE bigger things came, though always buffeted by storms of controversy. From 1872 to 1877, Standard went on acquiring docks, ships and plants throughout the nation—in Pittsburgh, Louisville, Philadelphia, Bayonne, Weehawken and in dozens of lesser towns. The Pennsylvania Railroad tried to fight Rockefeller through a subsidiary freight company called Empire Transportation. Empire hoped to get into refining, where it could use its railroad connections to good advantage. But Standard drove Empire to the wall, bought out its refining properties in 1877 and by 1878 was extracting from the Pennsylvania and all other roads the kind of rebates which the ill-fated South Improvement Company had sought.

A group of independents organized as the Petroleum Producers' Union pulled political wires in Pennsylvania in 1878 to bring suit against Standard and its railroad allies for conspiracy to secure a monopoly and restrain trade. Although the suits were later dismissed, Standard was obliged to make concessions that put a stop to some of the transportation discrimination practiced against independents. In 1879 the development of a trans-Allegheny pipeline gave independent petroleum producers who hated Standard a flicker of hope. Perhaps the big company's stranglehold on transportation to seaboard markets could be broken and the way opened for competition once more. But Standard itself created a pipeline subsidiary, slashed rates and finally broke the competing pipeline (run by the producers) by buying up the customers it served.

Standard's growth rate was staggering. In 1870 Rockefeller had produced 10 per cent of the refined petroleum manufactured in the entire country; by 1879 the figure for Standard was more than 90 per cent. The famous trust agreement was merely a necessary legal step to permit the administrative unification of dozens of former competitors that had been absorbed. Stockholders in the various refining, storage, sales, shipping and other merged companies that made up the new complex exchanged their holdings for shares of Standard Oil Trust. The nine-member board which held their surrendered certificates in trusteeship thus was clad with the technical authority to run the affairs of the business empire.

The device was widely and admiringly copied until, in the '80s, there were

John D. Rockefeller Sr., his body an oil barrel, looks out benignly from under his oil-lamp-shade hat. Dividing his time among Standard Oil, family and church, the "world's richest man" led a stern life. He spent hours with missionaries and educators, discussing the disposition of his fortune. At times, however, he sang at dinner or balanced a cracker on his nose.

trusts controlling the manufacture of cottonseed oil, whiskey, cordage and lead. Under attack in state courts for legal irregularities, the trust was replaced by an even more effective (and legally acceptable) method of combination, the holding corporation. This new entity was created exclusively for the purpose of owning controlling stock interest in other corporations. The form might change; the fact of consolidation was permanent.

B Y the mid-'80s Standard had become the synonym for monopoly, and Rockefeller a stereotype of the industrial czar. The official story of how he reached this pinnacle was presented by a Standard executive in 1888. "Our hold on this trade," he said, "is . . . the result of the application of better methods and of better business principles than have been brought against us." And, he added, those who complained of Standard's methods were "people who have failed through their lack of ability . . . and who would not succeed under any circumstances."

Much of Standard's formidable efficiency was due to John D. Rockefeller. By 1879 his frock-coated figure had a way of appearing in Standard offices and plants at unexpected times. His keen eyes peered out of a face strengthened by a large, reddish mustache, and those eyes were alert for the fraction-of-a-cent economy per barrel which, multiplied by thousands of barrels a day, added up to millions over the years. Perhaps it was picayune for the head of a multimillion-dollar concern to call an employee to account for a few missing barrel bungs, but even one of Rockefeller's modern critics has noted that "the spirit regarded as parsimony is a large-visioned concept of technical efficiency in handling big machines."

On the other hand, there was no denying the fact that Standard had been ruthless in using its power to harass competitors, to block their shipping routes, to woo away their suppliers, to threaten their customers. This was not merely a friendly race to market a superior product; this was industrial war. Its casualties were real. Indeed, the ruler of Standard himself named a principal victim when he looked back on the creation of the trust some years later. "The time was ripe for it," he said. "It had to come. . . . The day of combination is here to stay. *Individualism has gone*, never to return." It was a good, brief epitaph. Rockefeller did not waste words any more than money.

When Rockefeller used the word "individualism," he was referring to the small business firm, whose owner was content to rule in his little kingdom. Some men—men like Sam Andrews, Rockefeller's original partner in the refining business—could not understand that times had changed. Andrews was a ruddy, likable Englishman, a chemist and a mechanic who enjoyed the practical work of refining oil. As Standard grew and grew, Andrews felt increasingly out of touch with the organization he had helped found. The problems of big business held no allure for him. Finally, he sold his stock in the concern for one million dollars, lived to regret the decision when the shares ultimately became worth far more, and died fairly rich but not especially happy. Somehow, living on interest did not spice a man's life like a well-done (and profitable) job of tangible work.

But other men were at home with the Rockefeller way of business. There was James Buchanan Duke, for one, who organized the American Tobacco Company in 1890. This $25 million trust united the five leading cigarette firms in the country. In pursuit of Duke's goal of making "every style of tobacco

"Go Slow and Sure, and prosper then you must / With Fame and Fortune, while you Try and Trust," advised Horatio Alger Jr. in novels like "Luck and Pluck." Although he wrote over 100 books tracing the climb to success of clean-cut lads who left home to seek their fortune, Alger chose a path of pleasure that was neither slow nor sure. He died penniless.

the public wanted," the American Tobacco Company by 1900 was making over half the smoking tobacco, 62 per cent of the chewing tobacco and 93 per cent of the cigarettes produced in the United States—and piping the tune to which growers and retailers danced.

Like Standard, the tobacco trust won its victories through efficiency, advertising and arm-twisting. A dealer who sold a competitor's chewing tobacco, for example, got no American Tobacco Company cigarettes, which might be indispensable for holding his customers. And if a retailer were unco-operative, American Tobacco had a way of opening a retail store across the street.

Or there were the men like Henry O. Havemeyer. In 1887 he was a leading agent in organizing more than a dozen sugar refineries into a trust whose objectives were to keep sugar prices "as low as is consistent with reasonable profit," to share technical information, to "furnish protection against unlawful combinations of labor" and "generally to promote the interests" of the parties to the agreement. When questioned by a Congressional Committee on Manufactures, Havemeyer admitted that the trust employed some 25,000 out of 30,000 refining workers in the country, but he calmly insisted that the constituent companies were entirely free to compete with each other.

Public reaction was confused and confusing. The trusts fulfilled the American yearning for bigness and boldness. What was more, the over-all trend of prices in the "trustified" industries was downward—but not evenly, and not everywhere, and not entirely due, as everyone assumed, to the increased efficiency of the combinations. Technical progress and swelling markets also exerted their own downward push on costs.

The growing combines in telephone and telegraph services, farm machinery, meat packing, electrical equipment and other essential items were, beyond argument, rendering the services and achieving the expansion for which they were created. Nonetheless, the nation was not ready to share the satisfaction that Rockefeller took in declaring that "individualism has gone." The rhetoric of Jackson and Lincoln gave an important place to the words "equality" and "opportunity"—and admirable as the achievements of an integrated economy might be, they unquestionably reduced equality of independent opportunity, unless the definition could be stretched to include equality of the opportunity to go bankrupt by competing with the trusts.

The rise of a Gould, a Rockefeller or a Frick might delight those who enjoyed seeing a poor boy make good. Where, however, did the poor boys, grown to power in the land, fit into American society and government? What was to be done when their actions set the price of bread and meat, of light and warmth for millions? Combination had its sting as well as its honey. Could the two be separated?

STRUGGLING with its own contradictory attitudes, the public moved to meet the problem and found that economic abuses national in scope had to be met with national action. The railroads were first to feel the fire. Their powers were more obvious and more irritatingly used, and as common carriers they were considered quasi-public utilities. As early as 1871 combinations of unhappy farmers and shippers succeeded in pushing regulatory laws through the Illinois legislature. By 1874 Iowa, Minnesota and Wisconsin had passed similar acts. These measures usually provided for regulatory commissions, and prohibited rebates, discrimination between long- and short-haul rates,

Tobacco became big business in the three decades following the Civil War. One sign of the boom was the increase of the tobacconist's emblems, including the wooden Indian (above). Another was the phenomenal success of a brand of tobacco identified by the bull on its label (below). By 1880 "Bull Durham" was the best-selling smoking tobacco in this country.

135

John Sherman gave his name to the first U.S. antitrust act. Of the law for which Sherman is remembered, a senator said: "I do not think he ever understood it." The rumor was that he introduced the bill to spite an industrial baron who had blocked his presidential hopes. Far from radical, Sherman worked hard to resume specie payments—a de facto gold standard.

the bribing of public officials with free passes and the arbitrary and sudden alteration of rates. Because much of the initiative for this legislation came from the Patrons of Husbandry, the outspokenly antirailroad organization of farmers whose local chapters were called granges, the acts were known as "Granger laws."

The name has passed into history to mislead succeeding generations into thinking that early railroad regulation was the result of Midwestern agrarian discontent. The truth is less flattering to yeoman virtue. The advocates of regulation came in good part from cities and corporations that suffered under railroad abuses. Furthermore, several Eastern states in which farmers were not a potent political group—notably Massachusetts—simultaneously established railroad investigatory agencies.

The Granger laws were quickly challenged, but the Supreme Court sustained the Illinois statute in 1877. Nine years later, however, the court saw matters in a different light. In the case of the *Wabash, St. Louis and Pacific Railroad Co. vs. Illinois* it was held that the state could not regulate railroad charges within its borders if the offending line was involved (as all the significant ones were) in interstate transportation. It seemed that the power to regulate commerce among the several states was, after all, exclusively within the province of the federal government.

In 1890 in *Chicago, Milwaukee and St. Paul Railroad Co. vs. Minnesota*, the Supreme Court affirmed that the judicial officials of a state had the right to rule on the reasonableness of a railroad commission's rate orders; otherwise, said the court, corporations would be deprived of their property by the state without the due process of law guaranteed under the 14th Amendment. The railroads, as well as other corporations, were happy to have the matter of regulation left to the state courts, where the law's delays allowed plenty of time to discourage opponents, and expensive attorneys and political influence could earn their just rewards.

The Wabash and Minnesota Freight Rate cases, as they were popularly called, destroyed the foundations of state railroad regulation. Obviously, the next step was up to Congress. There was enough pressure there for regulation, even before the Minnesota decision, to push through the Interstate Commerce Act of 1887. This act created the five-man Interstate Commerce Commission, provided that rates should be just and reasonable, forbade sundry discriminations between localities and classes of freight, and outlawed pooling. The commission was empowered to proceed against violators in the federal courts. Subsequently, court decisions reduced this power. But the act was a first step, and it was important for what it promised rather than for what it could immediately achieve.

MEANWHILE, the general outcry against concentration continued to swell. Feeling ran so high that both the major parties were forced to make a bow in the direction of antimonopoly feeling in the election year of 1888. The Republican platform declared "opposition to all combinations of capital, organized in trusts or otherwise, to control arbitrarily the condition of trade among our citizens." The Democrats deplored "trusts and combinations . . . which . . . rob the body of our citizens by depriving them of the benefits of natural competition."

Confronted with such sentiments, the 51st Congress passed—and on July

2, 1890, President Benjamin Harrison signed—a historic piece of legislation, the Sherman Antitrust Act. It was a law full of almost comic paradoxes. It bore the name of John Sherman, brother to the famous general, senator from Ohio, sometime Cabinet member, occasional favorite son for the Republican nomination and all-round conservative—a man of far more honors than distinction. Though he introduced the bill, Sherman did not draft it. The act provided that "every contract, combination in the form of trust or otherwise, or conspiracy, in restraint of trade or commerce among the several States or with foreign nations" was illegal. In addition, it proclaimed that every person who should "monopolize or attempt to monopolize, or combine or conspire . . . to monopolize" interstate or foreign commerce should be guilty of a misdemeanor, and it directed the Attorney General of the United States to proceed against such malefactors.

The act, however, did not define trusts or conspiracies or monopolies. It was passed by the same Congress which three months later passed the stiffly protective McKinley Tariff, despite widespread admission that some trusts had grown to power behind the tariff shield. (The trust activities killed off domestic competition, and the national government destroyed foreign competition.) And lastly, the Sherman Act was the work of the 51st Congress, also dubbed the "Billion-Dollar Congress," a body solidly packed with friends of the great corporations whose activities were swiftly shrinking the area of free competition.

THE passage of the Sherman Act could have been dismissed as a cynical effort to make political hay with the minimum of damage to business, or, as Senator Orville Platt of Connecticut put it, to "get some bill headed 'A bill to punish trusts' with which to go to the country." Another, slightly more complex, explanation for the inconsistency might have been offered: the legislators felt instinctively that competition was a good thing and that it might, somehow, be restored by punishing trusts. The difficult job of determining punishment was left to the courts.

Neither the Interstate Commerce Act nor the Sherman Act had much effect upon the economy in their infant years. In fact, the decade of the '90s was to see a breathtaking increase in the pace of consolidation. Still, one thing had been done. The people acting through the Congress had, hesitantly but irrevocably, committed the federal government to intervening in the mysterious domain of economic transactions. In so doing, the people were asking the government to answer insoluble questions concerning economic justice and the possible means of reconciliation between a highly organized society and the free individual.

The American nation could accept neither limitless competition nor uncontrolled combination as the ultimate way of life in business. Nor would the country let the matter rest undecided without some expression of popular will, some precedent for acting to control the drift. Puny as they were, the Interstate Commerce Act and the Antitrust Act were blows at economic anarchy. Viewed in one perspective, they might seem to be gauzy veils flung over the problems of railroad and industrial consolidation—evanescent veils that would be shredded in the decade that followed. Seen at longer range, however, the laws would prove to be the first strands in a web that would harness the great corporations to the vehicle of the public interest.

Swathed in a motley big-business robe, the Statue of Liberty acclaims "the Home of the Trusts and the Land of the Plutocrats." In sharp contradiction to its true symbolism, the statue, blinded by avarice, ignores the vessel of "The People" foundering at her feet. Thomas Nast drew this cartoon in 1889 as a protest against the trusts and their control of many necessities.

Supposedly mirroring "languorous Oriental charm," a man's den shows the Victorian love of clutter.

The glitter of a tinseled elegance

Fᴏʀ a select handful of Americans, the last 25 years of the 19th Century meant affluence without precedent. Immense fortunes were made—in railroads, in oil and in exploiting the revolution in methods of production and distribution. Among these enormously wealthy Victorians, there was a craving to establish themselves in what they conceived to be baronial splendor. Invariably, this meant surrounding themselves with *things*—and the more things the better. The feeling was that if one *objet d'art* enhanced a room, another 500 made it irresistible. Indeed, the unchallenged arbiter of home decoration of the times declared: "Provided there is room enough to move about without walking over the furniture, there is hardly likely to be too much in a room!" Witness the elaborate den above: in this atmosphere of brocaded ostentation, everything was done to death. A simple table could scarcely carry the weight of its own knobby ornamentation, and windows were draped with so many curtains they often ceased to function as sources of light. Even the female body was clothed in all the fabric it could support. When it came to houses, the gingerbread was embellished with gingerbread *(right)*. Not surprisingly, people's emotions were frequently submerged under layers of artificiality. Courtship was marked by ritualized formality and prudishness, and class-conscious snobbery was assiduously cultivated—all at a time when the sweatshop system was demanding intolerably long hours.

GAUDY FUSSINESS adorns every last inch of this mansion, built in 1886 by a California lumberman. Its style might be called Neo-Gothic-Renaissance-Victorian-Americana.

138

DEMURE NYMPH, complete with wings, holds her lamp aloft amid a spray of cattails.

BRIC-A-BRAC, knickknacks, doohickeys and thingumbobs occupy the shelves of an 1880 whatnot. The items shown include: a showy trinket case *(fourth row up, left);* a porcelain shoe with spats *(second row up);* two plump tots in a ceramic bisque pannier *(center row);* an oil lamp and handlike vase *(bottom row).*

140

Even the bedroom of a Wisconsin fur trader, with its marquisette curtains and marble washstand, bows to the fussy décor of the times.

An uncontrollable mania for the absolutely useless

SOME historians manage to see in the showy tastes of the late 1800s an extension of the driving vitality which enabled the very wealthy to accumulate their riches in the first place. For most, however, all this ostentation added up to what Thorstein Veblen called "conspicuous consumption." Yet this does not detract from the respect owed Victorian designers for their ingenuity at finding ways to adorn even the most mundane objects with manifest opulence. What more, for example, could be done to ornament a baby carriage beyond what was achieved by the creator of the one at the right? And it would take some doing to surpass the lamp *(far left)* as the means simply to support one light bulb. However, if inspiration lagged, a designer could always fall back on the ever-popular cupid (on the mantel above), without which no home seemed really complete. But even more vital was the bric-a-brac stand *(left)*, for the display of such indisputably inane items as mother-of-pearl trinket cases for the storage of more gimcracks.

ORNATE BABY BUGGY, with its elaborate woven scrollwork and organdy parasol, is the antithesis of functional design. But its real function was to attract attention, and it served that well.

141

Apotheosis of gentility

Family Group is the patently obvious title of this cozy scene of wealthy home life in the latter 19th Century. It depicts Alfrederick Smith Hatch and his closest kin in their Park Avenue home in New York. Actually very little is known about the Hatch family, but this elaborate portrait has become justly

famous as an authentic representation of Victorian domesticity. Mrs. Hatch, mother of the 11 Hatch children, leans fetchingly against the mantel. Mrs. Ruggles, Mrs. Hatch's mother, tends to her own knitting, while Mr. Hatch at his desk quizzically observes young John about to escape through the door. Somehow, in the crimson-draped gloom characteristic of Victorian homes, old Dr. Horace Hatch manages to find enough light to read his newspaper. The canvas was painted by Eastman Johnson in 1871. Johnson was so popular that he is said to have received $1,000 for each member of the family, baby included.

NONCONTROVERSIAL PAINTING by Frank Waller shows a gallery of New York City's Metropolitan Museum of Art when it was still located in a private house. The museum directors' policy countenanced respectable banality. Offered the statue of a dancing girl, the president warned: "Hereafter we must curb the exuberance of donors except in the article of money."

144

The importance of being artistically respectable

LIKE puritans before and since, the Victorians preached "morality" and practiced intolerance. Nowhere was this more evident than in the field of art. Painters and sculptors were "good" if they conformed to accepted standards and "bad" if they rebelled. These standards, of course, were established by those wealthy enough to be patrons—and they were the very people who were busy filling flashy mansions with bric-a-brac. To escape this situation, many gifted American artists, among them James Whistler and John Singer Sargent, went abroad. Of those who remained, most turned out work of dreary conformity (left). But there were a few defiantly refreshing exceptions who stayed home. One was Thomas Eakins, whose work is shown on this page.

CONDEMNED FOR NUDITY, Eakins' work shows a model posing for a sculptor. Though its realism recalled Rembrandt, the fact that it portrayed an actual scene was thought scandalizing.

CONTROVERSIAL FOR ITS REALITY, this portrait of *The Concert Singer* shows Eakins' penchant for detail. But by Victorian standards, it is too lifelike—the lady has throat muscles.

BASEBALL poster advertises the Giants in 1887. Professional games began in 1869 and, at first, attempts were made to restrict attendance to the upper classes. Thus this lithograph ignored the shirt-sleeved fans who made the game the national sport.

TENNIS, a tasteful game and refined enough to discourage the riffraff, draws this mildly enthusiastic turnout in the 1880s. The young lady in the foreground is about to make a ladylike forehand return of a well-mannered lob shot delivered by the opposition.

COACHING enthusiasts in this handsome four-in-hand enjoy a Sunday drive in Philadelphia. Though ostensibly a refreshing outdoor sport for "sedentary citizens," coaching also just happened to provide a chance to show off one's finery and carriage. It was common knowledge that the cost to buy and operate a rig like the one above was only a little over $20,000 a season.

Irreproachable outdoor sport for a parvenu society

IT was no simple matter for a well-to-do Victorian to find an acceptable excuse to leave the upholstered sepulcher he called his home and venture into the out-of-doors. The trouble lay in finding an outdoor activity that was suitably genteel—a term that obviously implied something not engaged in by the lower classes. For the ladies, there was the additional concern over the use and possibly disfiguring development of their muscles—not to mention the fearsome possibility of sunburn. Coaching (*above*) qualified, of course, since it was delightfully showy, obviously expensive and hardly even tiring. When baseball (*upper left*) caught on with the masses, the upper crust promptly dropped it in favor of archery (*right*) and later tennis. Who could resist a sport described as being "far too refined a game to offer any attractions for the lower orders of society"?

ARCHERY, a highly acceptable pastime, entices these young ladies to an 1880 New York match. Rivalry was "keen to the last degree," but "refinement and courteous dignity" prevailed.

The conservative exterior of The Breakers only hints at the riches inside. Amazingly, it was built in only two years—but cost was no object.

A palace by the sea for a ferryman's grandson

IT was probably inevitable that among the affluent Victorian Americans determined to create the ultimate in residential palaces, somebody would finally succeed. And who was better equipped for success than a Vanderbilt? It was Cornelius, grandson of the ferryman-to-financier Cornelius, who converted four million dollars into a 70-room "cottage," as the elite termed all summer homes. Set on an 11-acre promontory at Newport, Rhode Island, the mansion was named The Breakers and the over-all effect, succinctly put by one observer, was "paralyzing." Two of its largest rooms were designed and built in France, torn apart, shipped to Newport and carefully rebuilt by French workmen brought over for that purpose. In addition to the standard accouterments, its bathrooms had hot and cold running *salt* water. Completed in 1895, The Breakers became a mecca for high society. Another Vanderbilt, William K., owned the nearby Marble House, amidst whose comparable splendor was announced the engagement of his daughter Consuelo to a titled Englishman. The Vanderbilts got a duke; the duke got $2.5 million plus $100,000 a year.

A PALATIAL ROOM, the dining hall towers two stories high and extends 58 feet. It is dominated by two massive crystal chandeliers. The table, set here for 10, could be extended to seat 34.

A MAGNIFICENT CATCH, the Duke of Marlborough looms small beside Consuelo Vanderbilt in this caricature. The marriage of American money and English nobility ended in bitterness.

Flamboyant Victorians
turned stuffy by posterity

Wıтн the passing years, the Victorian Era has come to be synonymous with sedate gentility. Almost nothing could be further from the truth. Some few acquired wealth "outrivaling all previous achievements in the history of lucre." They spent it the same way—on cigarettes wrapped in $100 bills, on oysters graced with black pearls. Indeed, far from being sedate, it was a flamboyant era—and even the masses delighted in observing it. Will there ever be another such time of uninhibited tastelessness—and unlimited tax-free funds?

A BILLIARD ROOM at The Breakers, in manly motif, has marble walls and a light fixture recalling the Middle Ages. The weighing chair (*foreground*) reads weight in English stones.

THE GRAND SALON is one of two rooms from France. Here were held various functions, attendance at which was the sure sign of everybody who was anybody in society.

CHRONOLOGY *A timetable of American and world events: 1877-1890*

WORLD EVENTS	EXPANSION and EXPLORATION	POLITICS	MILITARY and FOREIGN AFFAIRS	ECONOMICS and SCIENCE	THOUGHT and CULTURE
1877 Queen Victoria proclaimed empress of India	1877 Desert Land Act encourages irrigation of arid areas	1877 Special electoral commission declares Hayes President	1877 Nez Percé Indians, under Chief Joseph, defeated	1877 Nationwide railroad strikes	1877 Foundation of American Humane Association
1877 British annexation of Transvaal	1878 Timber and Stone Act opens timber rights on public domain to settlers	1877 End of vestiges of Reconstruction in the South	1877 H. O. Flipper is first Negro graduate of West Point	1877 Asaph Hall discovers the moons of Mars	1877-94 Romanesque revival in architecture
1877 Tolstoy's *Anna Karenina* published	1878 Powell report on explorations in Western arid regions	1877 Supreme Court upholds state Granger laws directed against railroad abuses	1877 Federal troops used to put down railroad strikes	1878 First general assembly of Knights of Labor	1877-99 Dwight Moody and Ira Sankey at height of their Protestant evangelism
1877-1911 Diaz dictatorship in Mexico	1878-85 Land boom in the Dakotas	1877 Socialist Labor party formed	1877-80 Army authorized to pursue Mexican bandits across Mexican border	1878 Michelson determines the velocity of light	1877 onward Beginnings of modern American sculpture
1878 Treaties of San Stefano and Berlin end Russo-Turkish war	1878-93 Hill's Great Northern Railway built from St. Paul to Seattle	1877 California Nativists form Workingmen's party	1878 Joint Commission recommends army retrenchment	1878 Edison patents the phonograph, perfected in 1888	1878 American Bar Association formed
1878-90 Socialist activities outlawed in Germany	1879 U.S. Geological Survey established	1878 Bland-Allison Act requires silver purchases by government	1879 Ute Indians stage abortive uprising	1879 Edison invents first practical incandescent bulb	1878 First bicycle manufactured in the U.S.
1878-1903 Pontificate of Leo XIII	1879 Hayes vetoes restriction of Chinese immigration	1878-84 Greenback Labor party of inflationists and reformers	1879 National Guard Association formed	1879 Billings establishes the *Index Medicus*	1879 Mary Baker Eddy establishes Church of Christ, Scientist
1878-1960 British rule in Cyprus	1879 Creation of Public Land Commission	1879 Resumption of specie payments			1879 George's *Progress and Poverty* published
1879 Formation of Austro-German Dual Alliance	1879-81 Failure of De Long expedition to North Pole	1879-81 Democrats control both houses for the first time since 1858			1879 Women win right to practice before the Supreme Court
1879 De Lesseps organizes Panama Canal Company					
1879 Ibsen's *A Doll's House* published					

1880 Fifty Million Americans

WORLD EVENTS	EXPANSION and EXPLORATION	POLITICS	MILITARY and FOREIGN AFFAIRS	ECONOMICS and SCIENCE	THOUGHT and CULTURE
1880 France expels Jesuits	1880 Census shows 50,155,000 inhabitants	1880 Exclusion of Negroes from jury duty held unconstitutional	1880 Treaty with China gives U.S. right to regulate "coolie" immigration	1880 93,262 miles of railway in the U.S.	1880 Lew Wallace's *Ben Hur* published
1880 Dostoevsky's *The Brothers Karamazov* published	1880 First major gold strike in Alaska	1880 Organization of National Farmers' Alliance	1880 William Sherman says: "War is . . . hell."	1880 U.S. surpasses Great Britain in production of steel	1880 Organization of U.S. branch of Salvation Army
1880-84 Stanley explores the Congo Basin	1881 Helen Hunt Jackson's *A Century of Dishonor* censures U.S. Indian policy	1880 Republicans split into "stalwart" and "half-breed" factions	1880 Hayes warns that any Isthmian canal must be under U.S. control	1880-90 Industrial expansion in the South	1880 Opening of the Metropolitan Museum of Art
1880-85 Second Gladstone ministry in England	1881-84 Greeley expedition to Arctic reaches lat. 83°24' N.	1880 Special Republican anti-third-term convention held to block Grant nomination bid	1881 Blaine attempts closer commercial ties with Latin America	1881 Formation of Federation of Organized Trades and Labor Unions	1880 Harris publishes his first *Uncle Remus* tales
1881 Alexander II of Russia assassinated	1881-87 Midwestern land boom	1880 James A. Garfield elected President			1880-1910 Impressionism influences American painting
1881 Formation of Austro-Serbian alliance	1881-90 5,246,613 immigrants enter U.S.	1881 Defeat of Conkling marks decline of "stalwart" faction			1881 Henry James's *The Portrait of a Lady* published
1881 French establish protectorate in Tunis	1882 Congress imposes 50 cent head tax on immigrants	1881 Garfield assassinated; Chester Arthur becomes President	1882 U.S. subscribes to Geneva Convention, setting rules for care of wounded in wartime	1882 Tesla discovers the rotating magnetic field	1881 Carnegie first offers to build libraries
1881 Pasteur applies vaccination principle to anthrax		1881 Court declares imposition of 1862 income tax law was constitutional	1882 Exclusion Act bars Chinese laborers	1882 First Labor Day celebration in New York City	1881 Whitman's *Leaves of Grass* withdrawn from sale in Boston
1881 onward Jewish pogroms in Russia		1882 Tariff Commission recommends drastic downward revision of imposts		1882 First U.S. hydroelectric plant	1881 Boston Symphony Orchestra founded
1882 Triple Alliance of Austria, Germany, Italy established					1881 American Red Cross organized
1882 British occupy Egypt					1882 Foundation of Tuskegee Institute
1882 Wagner's *Parsifal* completed					1882 John L. Sullivan wins heavyweight championship
1882 Koch discovers tuberculosis germ					
1882 St. Gotthard tunnel completed between Italy and Switzerland					

1883 London Fabian Society founded

1883 Stevenson's *Treasure Island* published

1883 Koch discovers cholera germ

1883-85 Foundation of German colonial empire

1885 Zola's *Germinal* published

1885 Daimler develops internal combustion engine

1883 Northern Pacific Railroad reaches the Pacific Coast

1883 Donaldson Report on abuses of land laws

1883-86 Gold rush in Idaho

1884 Federal troops disperse illegal Oklahoma settlers

1884 Alaska given rudiments of civil government

1885 Congress prohibits importation of contract labor

1885 Congress prohibits unauthorized fencing of public lands

1885-87 End of the cattle boom

1885-1914 Increase in number of immigrants from Southern and Eastern Europe

---

1883 Pendleton Act reforms civil service, establishes Civil Service Commission

1883 Court finds 1875 Civil Rights Act unconstitutional

1884 Republican nomination of Blaine causes "Mugwump" bolt to Cleveland

1884 Grover Cleveland elected President

1884-88 Suffragettes form Equal Rights party, nominate woman candidate for President

1884-96 Resurgence of agrarian political discontent

1885 Post Office establishes special delivery service

1885 Cleveland recommends suspension of silver-dollar coinage

---

1883 Congress authorizes first steel navy vessels

1884 Naval War College established at Newport

1884 U.S. participation in Red Cross International Congress

1885 Cleveland withdraws Frelinghuysen-Zavala canal treaty with Nicaragua from Senate

1885-88 Strained relations with Britain over Canadian fisheries

---

1883 Railroads inaugurate standard time zones

1883 Completion of the Brooklyn Bridge

1884 American Institute of Electrical Engineers founded

1884 Waterman perfects the fountain pen

1884 Creation of U.S. Bureau of Labor

1884 Eastman patents roll film

1884 Trudeau opens Saranac Lake Sanitarium

1884 Mergenthaler invents Linotype

1884-85 Development of cocaine as surgical anaesthetic

1885 Chicago's Home Insurance Building inspires term "skyscraper"

1885 American Economic Association founded

1885-86 Peak of Knights of Labor strength

1883 Opening of the New York Metropolitan Opera House

1883 "Buffalo Bill" Cody forms first Wild West show

1884 Twain's *Huckleberry Finn* published

1885 Leland Stanford University chartered

1885 Howells' *The Rise of Silas Lapham* published

1885 Dedication of the Washington Monument

1886 Gold rush in the Transvaal

1886 Heads of former reigning families banished from France

1886 First Irish Home Rule bill

1886 Poll tax abolished in Russia

1887 Queen Victoria's Golden Jubilee

1887 Attempted Boulanger coup in France a failure

1888 Launching of Berlin-Baghdad railway plan

1888 Nansen makes first crossing of Greenland

1888-1918 Wilhelm II kaiser of Germany

1889 Japan adopts constitution

1889 Brazil becomes a republic

1889 Completion of Eiffel Tower

1889 Formation of the Second Socialist International in Paris

1890 Bismarck dismissed as German chancellor

1886 Division of Forestry created within Department of Agriculture

1887 Reforms of the Land Commission revoked

1887 Dawes Act dissolves Indian tribes as legal entities and provides for apportionment of tribal lands among Indians

1889 North Dakota, South Dakota, Montana and Washington statehood

1889 Oklahoma land rush as territory is opened for settlement

1889 Sioux cede nine million acres to U.S.

1890 Idaho and Wyoming statehood

1890 Census bureau announces "end" of Western frontier

1890 Census shows 62,947,714 inhabitants

1890 All unutilized railroad land grants declared forfeit and returned to public domain

---

1886 Anarchists tried for Haymarket Massacre

1886-1947 Presidential Succession Act provides for succession of Cabinet members in event of death of President and Vice President

1887 Electoral Count Act passed to prevent repetition of 1876

1887 Interstate Commerce Commission first federal regulatory agency

1887 Cleveland vetoes pension bill

1887 Tenure of Office Act of 1867 repealed

1888 First use of Australian secret ballot in local elections

1888 Benjamin Harrison elected President

1888 New Jersey authorizes incorporation of holding companies

1890 Supreme Court reverses itself on Granger cases, restricts state regulatory power

1890 Sherman Antitrust Act passed

1890 McKinley tariff, highest yet adopted

1890 Sherman Silver Purchase Act replaces Bland-Allison Act

1890 Mississippi inaugurates new Southern policy of Negro disfranchisement

---

1886 Capture of Geronimo marks end of Plains Indian warfare

1887 Hawaii grants U.S. exclusive rights to have coaling station at Pearl Harbor

1887-99 U.S. attempts to mediate British-Venezuelan dispute

1888 Tacit U.S.-British agreement on Canadian fisheries

1888 British ambassador's election comments arouse Anglophobia

1889 First Pan-American Conference held

1890 Organization of the United Confederate Veterans

1890 U.S. signs agreement for suppression of African slave trade

1890 "Ghost Dance" war of Dakota Sioux

1890 Sitting Bull captured and killed

1890 Mahan's *The Influence of Sea Power upon History* published

---

1886 American Federation of Labor organized

1886 Completion of rail-gauge standardization

1886 Nationwide May Day demonstrations for eight-hour day

1887 Formation of the whiskey and sugar trusts

1887 Experimental agricultural stations set up under Hatch Act

1887 Severe drought in Midwest ends period of agricultural prosperity

1888 Establishment of Marine Biological Laboratory

1888 First successful electric trolley line inaugurated

1888 First Kodak hand camera developed

1888 Tesla patents the induction motor

1888 New York is first state to adopt electrocution as capital punishment

1888 Burroughs receives adding machine patent

1889 Department of Agriculture given Cabinet status

1889 Mayo Clinic founded

1889 Dickson and Eastman develop movie film

1890 Estimated 603,000 children between 10 and 14 at work in U.S.

1890 Duke's American Tobacco Company achieves virtual monopoly

1890 Creation of Weather Bureau

1886 Statue of Liberty unveiled in New York harbor

1886 Burnett's *Little Lord Fauntleroy* published

1886 First American settlement house opens in New York

1887 Bronson Howard's *Shenandoah*, first successful Civil War drama, performed

1888 Bellamy's *Looking Backward* published

1888 First public recitation of "Casey at the Bat"

1888 Formation of the Amateur Athletic Union

1888 Bryce's *The American Commonwealth* published

1888 New York City paralyzed by blizzard

1889 Formation of Sons of the American Revolution

1889 Walter Camp selects first All-America football team

1890 General Federation of Women's Clubs founded

1890 First Army-Navy football game, won by Navy

1890 U.S. illiteracy rate estimated at 13.3 per cent

1890 First printing of collected poems of Emily Dickinson

1890 Mormon Church ends approval of polygamy

FOR FURTHER READING

These books were selected for their interest and authority in the preparation of this volume, and for their usefulness to readers seeking additional information on specific points. An asterisk (*) marks works available in both hard-cover and paperback editions; a dagger (†) indicates availability only in paperback.

GENERAL READING

Butterfield, Roger, *The American Past.* Simon and Schuster, 1957.

Kirkland, Edward C., *Industry Comes of Age: Business, Labor and Public Policy, 1860-1897.* Holt, Rinehart & Winston, 1961.

Malone, Dumas, and Basil Rauch, *Empire for Liberty* (Vol. II). Appleton-Century-Crofts, 1960.

Miller, William, *The New History of the United States.* George Braziller, 1958.

Nevins, Allan, *Emergence of Modern America, 1865-1878,* Vol. VIII of History of American Life Series. Macmillan, 1927.

Parrington, Vernon L., *Main Currents in American Thought* (Vol. III). Harcourt, Brace & World, 1939.

Perkins, Dexter, and Glyndon G. Van Deusen, *The United States of America, a History* (2 vols). Macmillan, 1962.

Schlesinger, Arthur M., Sr., *The Rise of the City, 1878-1898,* Vol X of History of American Life Series. Macmillan, 1933.

Tarbell, Ida M., *Nationalizing of Business, 1878-1898,* Vol. IX of History of American Life Series. Macmillan, 1937.

White, Leonard D., *The Republican Era, 1869-1901.* Macmillan, 1958.

Woodward, C. Vann, *Origins of the New South, 1877-1913,* Vol. IX of History of the South. Louisiana State University Press, 1951.

REUNION POLITICS (CHAPTER 1)

Barnard, Harry, *Rutherford B. Hayes and His America.* Bobbs-Merrill, 1954.

Chidsey, Donald Barr, *The Gentleman from New York: A Life of Roscoe Conkling.* Yale University Press, 1935.

Flick, Alexander C., *Samuel Jones Tilden.* Dodd, Mead, 1939.

*Franklin, John Hope, *Reconstruction: After the Civil War.* University of Chicago Press, 1961.

*Hofstadter, Richard, *The American Political Tradition and the Men Who Made It.* Alfred A. Knopf, 1948.

*Josephson, Matthew, *The Politicos, 1865-1896.* Harcourt, Brace & World, 1940.

Muzzey, David S., *James G. Blaine: A Political Idol of Other Days.* Dodd, Mead, 1934.

Nevins, Allan, *Grover Cleveland; A Study in Courage.* Dodd, Mead, 1958.

Paine, Albert Bigelow, *Th. Nast, His Period and His Pictures.* Macmillan, 1904.

Randall, James G., and David Donald, *The Civil War and Reconstruction.* D.C. Heath, 1961.

Sharkey, Robert P., *Money, Class and Party, an Economic Study of Civil War and Reconstruction.* Johns Hopkins Press, 1959.

Werner, Morris R., *Tammany Hall.* Doubleday, Doran, 1928.

*Woodward, C. Vann, *Reunion and Reaction: The Compromise of 1877 and the End of Reconstruction.* Peter Smith, 1961.

THE ERA OF BIG BUSINESS (CHAPTERS 2, 6)

Allen, Frederick Lewis, *The Great Pierpont Morgan.* Harper & Row, 1949.

Andrews, Wayne, *The Vanderbilt Legend.* Harcourt, Brace & World, 1941.

Clark, Victor S., *History of Manufactures in the United States, 1607-1928* (Vol. II). Peter Smith, 1949.

†Cochran, Thomas C., and William Miller, *The Age of Enterprise: A Social History of Industrial America.* Harper Torchbooks, 1961.

Dolson, Hildegarde, *The Great Oildorado.* Random House, 1959.

Dulles, Foster Rhea, *America Learns to Play: A History of Popular Recreation, 1607-1940.* Peter Smith, 1952.

*Hays, Samuel P., *The Response to Industrialism: 1885-1914.* University of Chicago Press, 1957.

Hendrick, Burton J., *Life of Andrew Carnegie* (2 vols.). Doubleday, Doran, 1932.

Holbrook, Stewart H., *The Age of the Moguls.* Doubleday, 1953. *The Story of American Railroads.* Crown Publishers, 1947.

*Josephson, Matthew, *Edison.* McGraw-Hill, 1959. **The Robber Barons.* Harcourt, Brace & World, 1934.

Larkin, Oliver W., *Art and Life in America.* Holt, Rinehart & Winston, 1960.

Lewis, Oscar, *The Big Four.* Alfred A. Knopf, 1933.

Moody, John, *The Railroad Builders,* Vol. XXXVIII of Chronicles of America Series. Yale University Press, 1919.

*Mumford, Lewis, *The Brown Decades, a Study of the Arts in America, 1865-1895.* Peter Smith, 1960.

Nevins, Allan, *John D. Rockefeller.* Charles Scribner's Sons, 1959.

Seager, H. R., and C. A. Gulick, *Trust and Corporation Problems.* Harper & Row, 1929.

*Stover, John P., *American Railroads.* University of Chicago Press, 1961.

Swanberg, W. A., *Jim Fisk: The Career of an Improbable Rascal.* Charles Scribner's Sons, 1959.

Thorelli, Hans B., *The Federal Anti-Trust Policy.* Johns Hopkins Press, 1955.

Wecter, Dixon, *The Saga of American Society.* Charles Scribner's Sons, 1957.

CLOSING THE FRONTIER (CHAPTER 3)

Billington, Ray Allen, *Westward Expansion: A History of the American Frontier.* Macmillan, 1960.

Hamilton, James M., *From Wilderness to Statehood: A History of Montana, 1805-1900.* Binfords & Mort, 1957.

Lewis, Oscar, *The Silver Kings.* Alfred A. Knopf, 1947.

McCracken, Harold, *The Charles M. Russell Book.* Doubleday, 1957. *Frederic Remington, Artist of the Old West.* Lippincott, 1947.

†Osgood, Ernest Staples, *The Day of the Cattleman.* University of Chicago Press, 1957.

Sandoz, Mari, *The Cattlemen.* Hastings, 1958.

Shannon, Fred A., *The Farmer's Last Frontier: Agriculture, 1860-1897,* Vol. V of The Economic History of the United States. Holt, Rinehart & Winston, 1945.

*Swanberg, W. A., *Citizen Hearst.* Charles Scribner's Sons, 1961.

*Turner, Frederick Jackson, *The Frontier in American History.* Holt, Rinehart & Winston, 1959.

*Webb, Walter P., *The Great Plains.* Ginn, 1931.

THE CHALLENGE OF LABOR (CHAPTER 4)

Brody, David, *Steelworkers in America.* Harvard University Press, 1960.

Bruce, Robert V., *1877: Year of Violence.* Bobbs-Merrill, 1959.

Commons, John R., and others, *The History of Labour in the United States* (Vol. II). Macmillan, 1951.

David, Henry, *The History of the Haymarket Affair.* Russell and Russell, 1958.

Dulles, Foster Rhea, *Labor in America: A History.* Thomas Y. Crowell, 1960.

Gompers, Samuel, *Seventy Years of Life and Labor: An Autobiography* (ed. by Philip Taft and John A. Sessions). E. P. Dutton, 1957.

Harvey, Rowland Hill, *Samuel Gompers: Champion of the Toiling Masses.* Stanford University Press, 1935.

Powderly, Terence V., *The Path I Trod* (ed. by Harry J. Carman, Henry David and Paul N. Guthrie). Columbia University Press, 1940.

Ware, Norman J., *The Labor Movement in the United States, 1860-1895.* Peter Smith, 1959.

Yellen, Samuel, *American Labor Struggles.* Harcourt, Brace & World, 1936.

THE NEW SOUTH (CHAPTER 5)

*Buck, Paul, *The Road to Reunion, 1865-1900.* Peter Smith, 1959.

†Cable, George W., *The Negro Question* (ed. by Arlin Turner). Doubleday Anchor Books, 1958.

*Cash, Wilbur J., *The Mind of the South.* Alfred A. Knopf, 1960.

Dibble, Roy Floyd, *Albion W. Tourgée.* Lemcke & Buechner, 1921.

Franklin, John Hope, *From Slavery to Freedom: A History of American Negroes.* Alfred A. Knopf, 1956.

Hesseltine, William B., and David L. Smiley, *The South in American History.* Prentice-Hall, 1960.

Horn, Stanley F., *Invisible Empire: The Story of the Ku Klux Klan 1866-1871.* Houghton Mifflin, 1939.

Simkins, Francis B., *A History of the South.* Alfred A. Knopf, 1953.

Woodward, C. Vann, *Tom Watson, Agrarian Rebel.* Holt, Rinehart & Winston, 1955. **The Strange Career of Jim Crow.* Peter Smith, 1963.

ACKNOWLEDGMENTS

The editors of this book are particularly indebted to the following persons and institutions: David Brody, Assistant Professor, Columbia University; Albert K. Baragwanath, Museum of the City of New York; Paul Bride, The New-York Historical Society; Wilson Duprey, New York Public Library; Marston Alfred Hamlin and Sol Novin, Culver Pictures, Inc., New York City; Charles M. Garvey, Westinghouse Electric Corporation, New York City; Robert Heimann, American Tobacco Company, New York City; Roberts Jackson, The Bettmann Archive, New York City; Virginia Daiker, Milton Kaplan and Carl Stange, Library of Congress, Washington, D.C.; Wyatt Brummitt, Eastman Kodak Company, Rochester, New York; Kathleen Oliver, Norman Speiden and Melvin J. Weig, Edison National Historic Site, West Orange, New Jersey; Charles T. Haley, Hampton Institute, Hampton, Virginia; Mitchell A. Wilder, Amon Carter Museum of Western Art, Fort Worth, Texas; Jay P. Altmayer, Mobile, Alabama; Mary Lee Burke, William E. Groves and Alonzo Lansford, New Orleans, Louisiana; and Judy Higgins.

The author, for his part, wishes to extend his thanks to two research assistants, Jane Hobson and Lawrence Jorgensen.

PICTURE CREDITS

The sources for the illustrations in this book are shown below. Credits for pictures from left to right are separated by semicolons, top to bottom by dashes. Sources have been abbreviated as follows: Bettmann—The Bettmann Archive; Brown—Brown Brothers; Culver—Culver Pictures; LC—Library of Congress; N-YHS—The New-York Historical Society, N.Y.C.; NYPL—The New York Public Library.

Cover—Courtesy Museum of the City of New York.

End papers drawn by Thomas Vroman.

CHAPTER 1: 6—Courtesy of The White House. 8, 9—Bettmann. 10, 11—Culver; Bettmann. 12—NYPL. 13—Wide World Photos—Culver. 14, 15—Bettmann; from Stefan Lorant's *The Presidency*. 16, 17—Culver except top left Bettmann. 18 through 25—Culver. 26, 27—Left: Culver; right: NYPL.

CHAPTER 2: 28—Herbert Orth, courtesy The Union League Club, New York. 30—Culver. 31—Bettmann. 33 through 37—Bettmann. 38, 39—Edison National Historic Site, National Park Service; Herbert Orth, N-YHS. 40, 41—Left: Herbert Orth, Edison National Historic Site, National Park Service; right: Edison National Historic Site, National Park Service except top Bradley Smith, courtesy of Henry Ford Museum. 42, 43—Brown; Ohio Historical Society Library—Culver; AT&T Photo Service. 44, 45—Left: Culver—Bettmann; right: *Steelways*. 46, 47—Top left: George Eastman House; top right: Culver; center right: George Eastman House; bottom: N-YHS. 48, 49—Courtesy Museum of the City of New York.

CHAPTER 3: 50—Eliot Elisofon, artifacts from The Panhandle-Plains Historical Museum, Canyon, Texas. 52, 53—Bettmann except bottom left Bureau of American Ethnology, The Smithsonian Institution. 54—Culver. 56, 57—Cattle Brands of West Texas from the records of Fort Concho Museum, San Angelo, Texas; Stewart Holbrook Collection. 59—Culver. 60, 61—Erwin E. Smith photograph, courtesy LC and Mrs. L. M. Pettis; from the original oil painting in Woolaroc Museum, Bartlesville, Okla. 62, 63—Herbert Orth, from the permanent collection, Montana Historical Society, Helena; reprinted through courtesy of Brown & Bigelow, St. Paul, Minn.—Henry B. Beville, from the permanent collection, Montana Historical Society, Helena. 64 through 69—Erwin E. Smith photograph, courtesy LC and Mrs. L. M. Pettis. 70, 71—Courtesy Amon Carter Museum, Fort Worth, Texas; De Venny Wood Studio, courtesy Thomas Gilcrease Institute of American History and Art, Tulsa, Okla.

CHAPTER 4: 72—Courtesy of The White House. 74, 75—Bettmann except right Culver. 76, 77—Culver except left Brown. 78, 79—Bettmann; Culver. 80, 81, 82— Courtesy LC. 83—U.S. Signal Corps photo no. 111-5C-62958 in the National Archives. 84—Bettmann. 85, 86—Courtesy LC. 87—Culver. 88, 89—Culver except bottom left courtesy LC. 90, 91—Left: Culver; center: Brown; right: courtesy LC —Brown. 92, 93—Left: Culver; right: Brown (2). 94, 95—Culver except top right courtesy LC. 96, 97—Bettmann; Culver.

CHAPTER 5: 98—Henry B. Beville, courtesy Hampton Institute. 100, 101—Culver, Bettmann. 102, 103—Culver. 104—Bettmann. 105 through 110—Culver. 111—NYPL. 112, 113—Eric Schaal, Tulane University Library, New Orleans, La.; Eric Schaal, Pontalba House, Louisiana State Museum. 114, 115—Left: Bradley Smith—Eric Schaal, Isaac Delgado Museum of Art; right: Eric Schaal, collection of Alonzo Lansford. 116, 117—Left: Eric Schaal, Louisiana State University Library, Baton Rouge—Eric Schaal, collection of Alonzo Lansford; center and right: Eric Schaal, Isaac Delgado Museum of Art. 118, 119—Eric Schaal, Tulane University Library, New Orleans, La. 120, 121—Eric Schaal, The University of Southwestern Louisiana, Lafayette; Eric Schaal, collection of Alonzo Lansford—Eric Schaal, Tulane University Library, New Orleans, La. 122, 123—Photo Giraudon, Musée des Beaux-Arts, Pau, France; collection of Mr. and Mrs. John B. Bunker. 124, 125—Herbert Orth, collection of Prescott H. Rathborne.

CHAPTER 6: 126—Courtesy LC. 128, 129—Culver; Bettmann. 130, 131—Culver. 132, 133—Bettmann. 134—Culver. 135—Robert Kafka—The American Tobacco Company. 136, 137—Bettmann; NYPL. 138, 139—Photograph by Byron, The Byron Collection, Museum of the City of New York; Bradley Smith, courtesy The Ingomar Club, Eureka, Calif. 140—Bradley Smith; Dmitri Kessel. 141—Bradley Smith, bedroom in historic Villa Louis, Prairie du Chien, Wis., owned by the State Historical Society of Wisconsin—Bradley Smith. 142, 143—Herbert Orth, The Metropolitan Museum of Art, gift of Frederick H. Hatch, 1926. 144—Courtesy of The Metropolitan Museum of Art, purchase, 1895. 145—Thomas Eakins, *The Concert Singer* 1892, Philadelphia Museum of Art—Thomas Eakins, *William Rush carving his Allegorical figure of the Schuylkill River* 1877, Philadelphia Museum of Art. 146, 147—Fernand Bourges, courtesy LC; Thomas Eakins, *The Fairman Rogers Four-in-Hand* 1879, Philadelphia Museum of Art—Fernand Bourges, courtesy LC; Culver. 148, 149—© Arnold Newman except bottom right courtesy Sam Welles. 150, 151—© Arnold Newman.

155

INDEX

This symbol in front of a page number indicates a photograph or painting of the subject mentioned.

PRODUCTION STAFF FOR TIME INCORPORATED

Arthur R. Murphy Jr. (Vice President and Director of Production)
Robert E. Foy, James P. Menton, Caroline Ferri and Robert E. Fraser
Text photocomposed under the direction of Albert J. Dunn and Arthur J. Dunn

XX

Printed by The Safran Printing Company, Detroit, Michigan
Bound by Rand McNally & Company, Hammond, Indiana
Paper by The Mead Corporation, Dayton, Ohio
Cover stock by The Plastic Coating Corporation, Holyoke, Massachusetts

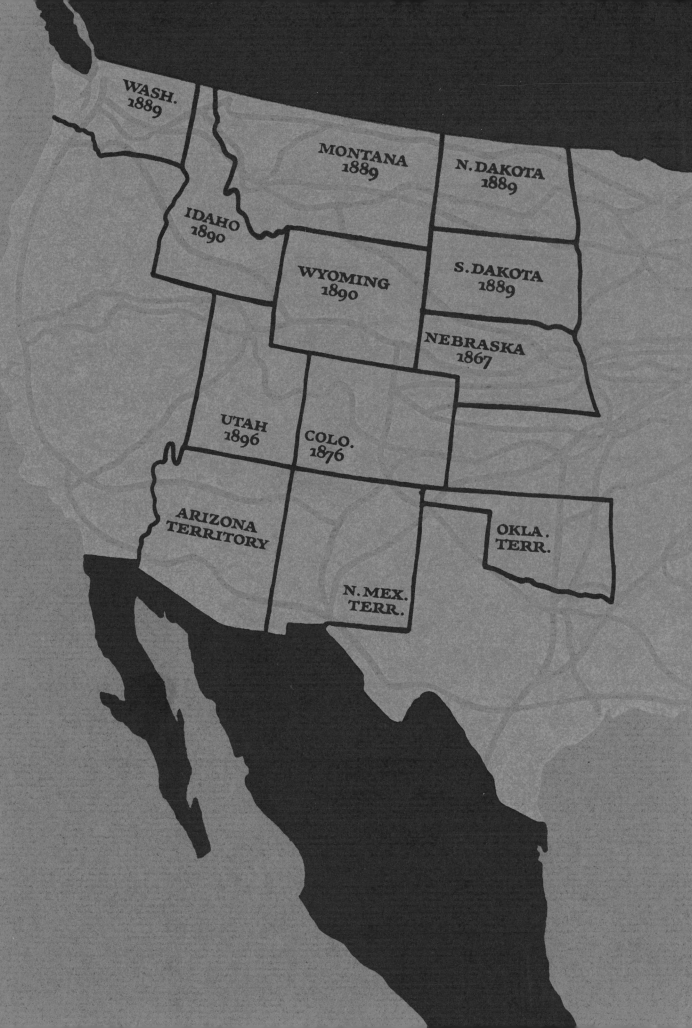